HEAT & ENERGY

1:1

answersingenesis

Petersburg, Kentucky, USA

3RD EDITION | **UPDATED, EXPANDED & FULL COLOR**

ANSWERS IN GENESIS **SCIENCE** BY DEBBIE & RICHARD LAWRENCE

God's Design® for the Physical World is a complete physical science curriculum for grades 3–8. The books in this series are designed for use in the Christian school and homeschool, and provide easy-to-use lessons that will encourage children to see God's hand in everything around them.

Third edition
Second printing August 2010

Copyright © 2008 by Debbie and Richard Lawrence

ISBN: 1-60092-156-6

Cover design: Brandie Lucas & Diane King
Interior layout: Diane King
Editors: Lori Jaworski, Gary Vaterlaus

The publisher and authors have made every reasonable effort to ensure that the activities recommended in this book are safe when performed as instructed but assume no responsibility for any damage caused or sustained while conducting the experiments and activities. It is the parents', guardians', and/or teachers' responsibility to supervise all recommended activities.

Published by Answers in Genesis, 2800 Bullittsburg Church Rd., Petersburg KY 41080

Printed in China

www.answersingenesis.org • www.godsdesignscience.com

PHOTO CREDITS

TABLE OF CONTENTS

WELCOME TO
GOD'S DESIGN®
FOR THE PHYSICAL WORLD

You are about to start an exciting series of lessons on physical science. *God's Design® for the Physical World* consists of three books: *Heat and Energy*, *Machines and Motion*, and *Inventions and Technology*. Each of these books will give you insight into how God designed and created our world and the universe in which we live.

No matter what grade you are in, third through eighth grade, you can use this book.

3rd–5th grade

Read the lesson and then do the activity in the ▬▬ box (the worksheets will be provided by your teacher). After you complete the activity, test your understanding by answering the questions in the ▬▬ box. Be sure to read the special features and do the final project.

6th–8th grade

Read the lesson and then do the activity in the ▬▬ box. After you complete the activity, test your understanding by answering the questions in the ▬▬ box. Also do the "Challenge" section in the ▬▬ box. This part of the lesson will challenge you to do more advanced activities and learn additional interesting information. Be sure to read the special features and do the final project.

There are also unit quizzes and a final test to take.

Throughout this book you will see special icons like the one to the right. These icons tell you how the information in the lessons fit into the Seven C's of History: Creation, Corruption, Catastrophe, Confusion, Christ, Cross, Consummation. Your teacher will explain these to you.

When you truly understand how God has designed everything in our universe to work together, then you will enjoy the world around you even more. So let's get started!

UNIT

1

FORMS OF ENERGY

FORMS OF ENERGY

It works!

LESSON
1

What is energy and what types of energy are there?

Words to know:

energy

mechanical energy

chemical energy

nuclear energy

thermal energy

electrical energy

magnetism

sound energy

light energy

Challenge words:

first law of thermodynamics

What do you think of when you hear the word *energy*? Do you think of running around the block or playing football? It certainly takes energy to perform physical activities. Maybe you think of the amount of gasoline it takes to drive a car. Your car needs energy to transport you from one place to another. Or maybe you thought of the energy needed to heat your home in the winter. All of these are examples of energy, but what is energy from a scientific point of view? The scientific definition of energy is the ability to perform work.

As you have already seen in the previous examples, there are many different types of energy. Energy is found in different forms, such as light, heat, sound, and motion. Although there are many forms of energy, they can all be put into two categories: kinetic and potential. Energy that is being used is called kinetic energy. Energy that is being stored is called potential energy. Forms of kinetic energy include mechanical, thermal, electrical, sound, and light energy. Forms of potential energy include chemical, nuclear, and gravitational energy. Each form of energy was designed by God to supply the energy needs of our world.

Mechanical energy is the energy of movement. When an object moves or has the potential to move, it is said to have mechanical energy. Movement of objects is quite often what we associate with work. Our car uses mechanical energy to move us from one place to another. A crane uses mechanical energy to pick up a giant iron beam. Most mechanical energy is produced when a different form of energy is converted into mechanical energy.

Chemical energy is energy that is stored or released during chemical reactions.

Chemical energy is associated with the energy levels of the electrons in atoms. As the electrons are forced into a higher energy level, they store energy. When they return to a lower energy level, they release energy. Photosynthesis and digestion are two of the most common chemical reactions that store and/or release chemical energy. Burning and combustion are also examples of the release of chemical energy.

Nuclear energy is also associated with the energy of atoms. However, nuclear energy is stored in the nucleus of the atom instead of the electrons. Nuclear energy can be released either by fission, which is the splitting of a nucleus into smaller particles, or by fusion, which is the combining of smaller particles to form a new nucleus. Tremendous amounts of energy are stored in the nuclei of atoms.

Thermal energy is also known as heat. It is the energy of moving atoms and molecules. Thermal energy is mechanical energy on an atomic or molecular scale. The more thermal energy an object's atoms contain, the higher its temperature will be. As the temperature goes up, the molecules or atoms move faster. As the molecules slow down, the temperature also goes down.

Electrical energy is the flow of electrons. Electrons can easily move through conductors such as copper and aluminum. This is the form of energy we use most often in our homes and buildings. When the electricity is shut off for some unexpected reason, it becomes very difficult to do many of the normal everyday activities because our society is very dependent on electricity.

Magnetism is a force you are probably familiar with. It is very closely related to electricity. Magnetism is basically a force between electric currents—two parallel currents in the same direction attract, and in opposite directions they repel. The earth itself has magnetic fields, most likely due to the flow of electrical ions in the planet's liquid outer core.

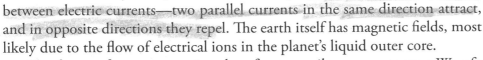

The forms of energy mentioned so far are easily seen as energy. We often see how electricity is used to make the various appliances in our homes work for us. We also know that if we put gas in our car, the chemicals in the gas are converted into mechanical energy. But, you may not associate sound and light with energy, because we do not see them producing work as readily as other forms of energy. Nevertheless, they are definitely forms of energy.

Sound energy is energy that travels in waves through matter such as air, water, or wood. The speed of the sound waves depends on the type of matter through which they are traveling. In general, most humans can detect sound waves that vibrate at frequencies between 20 and 20,000 vibrations per second (called Hertz). Many animals can hear sound waves at higher frequencies than humans can.

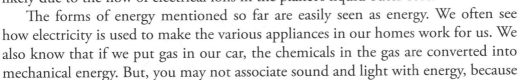

And finally, light energy is energy that also travels in

CONVERSION OF ENERGY

Energy is easily converted from one form to another. We need different kinds of energy for different functions. We need heat energy to warm our homes and cook our food. We need mechanical energy to wash our clothes and vacuum our carpets. We need light energy to light up our homes when the sun goes down. Many of these functions begin with electricity that enters our home and is then converted to the form in which we want to use it. To understand the many conversions that energy experiences, complete the "Energy Conversion" worksheet.

waves but does not need to move through a medium. Light is one form of electromagnetic radiation that can travel through empty space. Other forms of electromagnetic radiation include radio waves, infrared, ultraviolet, X-rays, and gamma rays. Light waves can travel through the vacuum of space at speeds up to 186,000 miles per second or about 300 million meters per second.

Probably the most important source of energy for the earth is the sun. The sun converts approximately 657 million tons of hydrogen into 653 million tons of helium every second! The remaining 4 million tons of matter are converted into energy including heat, light, and electrical energy. A portion of this energy travels across the vacuum of space to earth and heats and lights our world, providing the energy needed for photosynthesis and life. God has provided our world with many important sources of energy to more than adequately meet our needs. ■

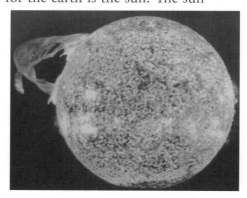

WHAT DID WE LEARN?

- What is the scientific definition of energy?
- What are some of the types of energy recognized by scientists?
- Which types of energy can be converted into other types of energy?

TAKING IT FURTHER

- Which types of energy are defined by the energy in the atoms or parts of atoms?
- Which types of energy can travel through space?
- If the sound of a solar flare was loud enough, could we hear it on earth?
- What is the final form of almost all energy?
- If most energy ends up lost, how do we keep everything working on earth?

ENERGY CHAINS

The **first law of thermodynamics** states that mass and energy cannot be created or destroyed; they can only change form. This is considered a scientific law because this is what has been observed time after time in scientific experiments. Energy is converted from one form to another, but no new energy is created in any known process. Since this is true, what is the ultimate source of all energy on earth?

Energy can easily change forms, so it is easy to trace the chain of energy in most processes. For example, let's look at the energy chain for a flashlight. At creation, God placed certain materials in the crust of the earth. Man extracts these materials and manufactures batteries. The batteries provide chemical energy that is converted into electrical energy. The electrical energy is converted inside the flashlight into light and heat.

Earth's crust => Mining of raw material => Manufacturing of batteries => Chemical energy => Electrical energy => Light and heat

This is a fairly simple energy chain. Other energy chains are more complex. On a copy of the "Energy Chains" worksheet, draw the energy chain for a coal-powered power plant. Include where the energy came from that is in the coal, and how the energy is used after it leaves the power plant.

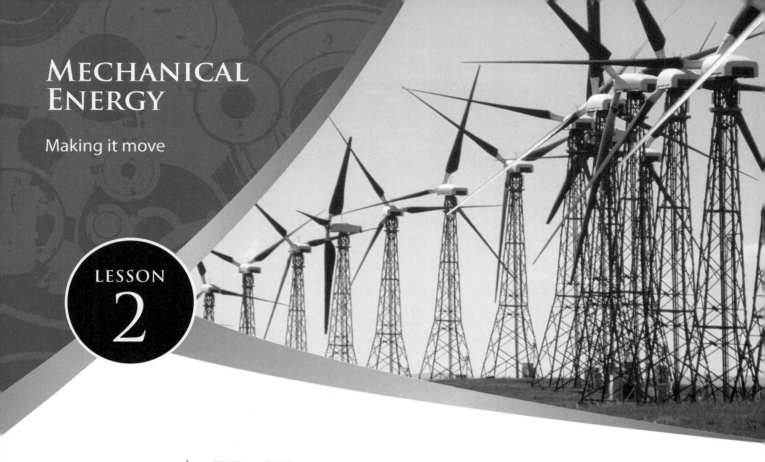

MECHANICAL ENERGY

Making it move

LESSON 2

What is mechanical energy and how do we use it?

Words to know:

kinetic energy

potential energy

Have you every seen pictures of an area that has been struck by a hurricane? The houses and trees are smashed and torn to pieces. This type of storm has a very large amount of mechanical energy. Mechanical energy is the energy possessed by moving objects or objects that have the potential to move. The wind and the water in a hurricane have a large amount of energy; therefore, they can cause a large amount of destruction. However, most mechanical energy is not used for destructive purposes. God has designed the world so that mechanical energy can be very beneficial to man, and man has become very ingenious in finding ways to harness this energy.

Hydroelectric plant

For example, the energy of water flowing down a mountain can be used in a hydroelectric plant to generate electricity. Similarly, man has been using the energy in wind to turn windmills for many different purposes. Windmills have

Some fun water energy facts:
- Water energy was used at least 2000 years ago when the Greeks used water to turn wheels to grind their grain.
- Water wheels became very popular during the industrial revolution when they were used for saw mills, to spin thread, and to run pumps.
- The first hydroelectric plant was built in the 1880s.
- One of the largest hydroelectric dam projects, Hoover Dam, was started in 1931 and is still in operation today.
- In 1940, about 40% of the electricity in the U.S. was generated by hydroelectric plants.
- Today, only about 7% of U.S. electricity is hydroelectric.
- About 60% of Canadian electricity is hydroelectric.

been used to grind grain, to generate electricity, and to run a pump that pumps water into animal water troughs. More recently, huge wind generators, like the ones shown at the beginning of this chapter, have been erected in areas that are frequently windy such as southern Wyoming. The wind turns the blades, which then turn turbines to generate electricity on a large scale.

Not all mechanical energy comes from nature. Obviously, God designed man and the animals to be able to move about. But many of the objects that contain mechanical energy were given that energy by human design. Man has designed a multitude of machines that perform work. From power tools to kitchen appliances, people enjoy the benefits of mechanical energy.

Mechanical energy can be found in two forms. If an object is moving, it has kinetic energy. A rock rolling down the hill is using its mechanical energy. A boy running across the yard is also using mechanical energy. But objects that have the potential to move also contain mechanical energy. The rock had mechanical energy before it started rolling down the hill. That energy was in the form of gravitational

OBSERVING MECHANICAL ENERGY

Purpose: To observe mechanical energy

Materials: two pennies

Procedure:

1. Place a penny on a table. Does the penny have any mechanical energy? You might be inclined to say no because the penny is not moving.

2. Push the penny toward the edge of the table until it falls off.

3. Now place the penny back on the table. Take a second penny and quickly slide it across the table so that it hits the first penny.

Questions:

- Did the penny have mechanical energy as it was falling?

- Did the penny have mechanical energy before it fell?

- How did the penny get the potential energy?

- What happened when the pennies collided?

- Explain where the mechanical energy came from and where it went.

HARNESSING WIND ENERGY

Purpose: To make your own windmill

Materials: piece of paper, straight pin, soda straw

Procedure:

1. Trace or photocopy the pattern below onto a piece of paper.

2. Carefully cut out and discard the white areas.

3. Gently fold all of the remaining "arms" toward the center, with the dark parts on the inside matching the dots to the center dot.

4. Tape each arm in place.

5. Stick a straight pin through the center and into a soda straw near one end of the straw. Now you can blow on the paper and watch it spin. This is the idea behind wind generators.

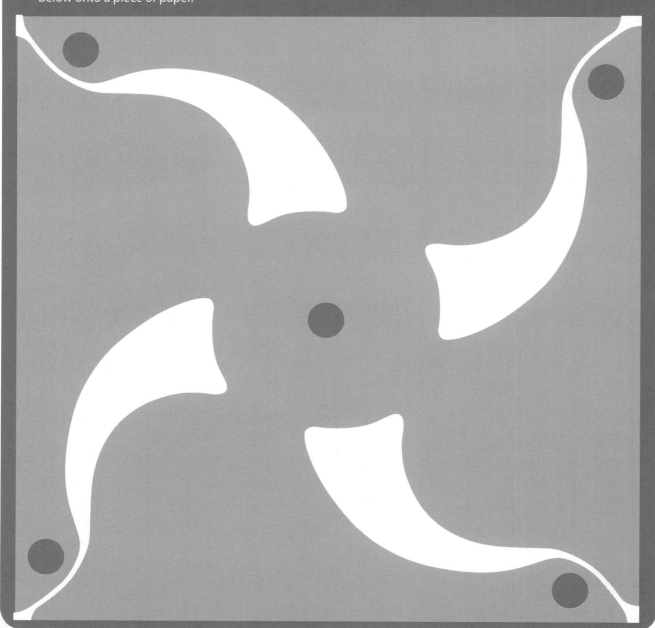

potential energy. Compressed or stretched springs also contain mechanical potential energy. As soon as the force holding them is released, the springs move back toward their natural state, thus releasing the mechanical energy.

Many of the principles of physics are based on the ideas of kinetic and potential energy. Because the scope of this book is to examine the various kinds of energy, these physical principles and ideas are covered in greater detail in the book *God's Design for Physical Science: Machines and Motion.* ■

WHAT DID WE LEARN?

- What is mechanical energy?
- What are the two forms of mechanical energy?
- What are some forces in nature that possess mechanical energy?

TAKING IT FURTHER

- Which has more potential energy, a book on the floor or a book on a table?
- List at least three ways that machines designed by humans use mechanical energy to make your life easier.
- When does a roller coaster have the most and the least potential energy?
- Give another example of potential energy being converted into kinetic energy.

POTENTIAL ENERGY

Purpose: To understand the role of height in potential energy

Materials: marble, books, cardboard or wood, "Potential Energy" worksheet

Procedure:

1. Using books and a piece of cardboard or wood, construct a ramp on the floor that is 1 inch high and 10 or more inches long.

2. Release a marble from the top of the ramp and let it roll down the ramp and across the floor until it stops. Measure how far the marble rolled. Record your measurements on a copy of the "Potential Energy" worksheet.

3. Now, add one or more books to raise the height of the ramp to 2 inches.

4. Again, let the same marble roll from the top of the ramp down and across the floor until it stops. Measure how far the marble rolled this time.

5. Repeat the experiment with a ramp that is 3 inches high. Measure how far the marble rolled from this taller ramp.

Conclusion: The marble rolls farther from a higher starting point because it possesses more potential energy than it did at a lower starting point.

CHEMICAL ENERGY

What did you eat today?

LESSON 3

What is chemical energy and how do we use it?

Words to know:

photosynthesis

cellular respiration

digestion

fossil fuels

combustion

Challenge words:

bioenergy

Chemical energy is the energy stored in the bonds of molecules. Energy is stored in molecules during certain chemical reactions and released during other chemical reactions. One of the most critical chemical reactions is photosynthesis. God has designed most plants so that a chemical reaction takes place inside the leaves. Carbon dioxide and water molecules inside the leaf combine to form sugar and oxygen molecules in the presence of sunlight and chlorophyll. Some energy from the sunlight is stored in the bonds of the sugar molecules.

As amazing as this process is, it would be useless if God had not also designed plants and animals to be able to break down the sugar molecules and release that stored energy for their own use. This process is called cellular respiration or digestion. The complementary processes of photosynthesis and digestion, along with the sun to provide the needed energy, are some of the most obvious examples of God's care for us.

There are many other examples of chemical energy as well. Many of the fuels that we use today are forms of chemical energy. Petroleum, which is the oil that gasoline and many other products are made from, is a carbon-based material that has energy stored in its molecules. When such materials are heated and burned, the energy is released. Coal is another carbon-based material that contains energy in its chemical bonds. Burning coal releases this energy in the form of heat and light. Coal and petroleum are called fossil fuels because they are formed from the remains of plants and animals that have been buried and placed under pressure. Most of these fossil fuels were formed as a result of the Genesis Flood. Candles, kerosene, and any other material that can burn also contain chemical energy that can be released through combustion or the process of burning.

HUNTING FOR CHEMICAL ENERGY

Complete the "Chemical Energy Scavenger Hunt."

Chemical energy plays a vital role in our lives. Not only does chemical energy provide our bodies with the energy for life, but chemical energy provides energy for most of our transportation and electricity needs. Most vehicles use some form of petroleum. Many new vehicles are switching to alternative fuels such as hydrogen fuel cells or electric batteries. But both hydrogen cells and battery cells produce mechanical energy by way of a chemical reaction. Also, many of the electric power plants burn coal to generate electricity. Thus, without chemical energy, much of the technology we have today would be useless. ■

WHAT DID WE LEARN?

- What is chemical energy?
- What two complementary processes were designed by God to change the sun's energy into energy for all living things?
- Name two fossil fuels.
- Other than digestion, what is the most common way to release chemical energy?

TAKING IT FURTHER

- Name two non-fossil fuels used in some automobiles and explain why they are chemical forms of energy.
- Why are people looking for alternatives to fossil fuels?
- Describe one way that chemical energy is used to produce electrical energy on a large scale?

BIOFUELS

Bioenergy is energy that comes from plant and animal matter. Bioenergy, therefore, is chemical energy that is stored in the molecules of the plants and animals. Ultimately, this chemical energy comes from the sun as plants convert the sun's energy into food.

One of the oldest forms of bioenergy is wood. People have been burning wood for fuel for thousands of years. People in many areas burn peat, which is decayed plant matter, instead of wood. Others have used animal waste as fuel. People have also used seal and whale blubber as oil for oil lamps. You can see that bioenergy is not new.

However, in recent years a new interest in biofuels has developed as we see our supplies of fossil fuels dwindling. Biofuels are considered renewable, whereas fossil fuels are not considered renewable.

Learn more about the new biofuels. Choose one or more of the following topics and research what that fuel is, how it is made, what it is used for, etc. Share your results with your class or family.

New biofuels: ethanol, biodiesel, methane, methanol, landfill gases.

NUCLEAR ENERGY

Using atoms

LESSON 4

What is nuclear energy and how do we use it?

Words to know:

fission

fusion

Challenge words:

radioactive

alpha particle

beta particle

gamma radiation

Nuclear energy is energy derived from the nucleus of an atom. It is also called atomic energy. Nuclear energy is released when protons or neutrons in the nucleus are rearranged. Although chemical and nuclear energy are both stored in the atoms, nuclear energy is millions of times more powerful than chemical energy.

Nuclear energy is a fairly recent discovery. A scientist named Enrico Fermi performed the first nuclear reaction at the University of Chicago in 1942. Since that time, much has been learned about the power of the nucleus, and the first nuclear power plant was built in England in 1956.

Nuclear power is different from other forms of energy. First, nuclear energy is much more powerful than other forms. Also, nuclear energy actually converts mass into energy. Albert Einstein demonstrated this in his research and defined this idea in his famous equation $E = mc^2$, which shows that energy is equal to mass times the speed of light squared. This equation explains how the sun can convert hydrogen to helium and release such vast amounts of energy. The sun converts over 4 million tons of mass into energy each second.

Nuclear energy is released through one of two different processes. The first process is called fission. Fission occurs when the nucleus of an atom is split apart into two smaller nuclei. Uranium is the primary element used for fission. Its nucleus is unstable and is easily split when hit by a fast moving neutron. This reaction produces more neutrons, which in turn hit other nuclei resulting in a chain reaction that can release extreme amounts of energy. This chain reaction can be controlled and is the method used to generate electricity in nuclear power plants.

The second process for a nuclear reaction is fusion. This is the combining of two nuclei or protons and neutrons to form a new, larger nucleus. Fusion only

MODELING A NUCLEAR POWER PLANT

Purpose: To understand how a nuclear power plant produces electricity

Materials: modeling clay

Procedure: Use modeling clay to make your own model of a nuclear power plant. If you have more than one color of clay, be sure to show that the reactor water is separated from the steam generator water. Use this diagram as a sample of how a nuclear power plant works.

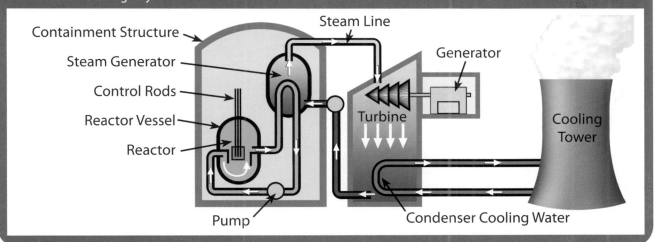

occurs at very high temperatures such as those found on the sun. Two hydrogen nuclei fuse to form one helium atom. Fusion produces more energy than fission, with less radioactive waste. If fusion could be performed at lower temperatures, it would have the potential to be the energy source of the future, but this is unlikely.

Since low-temperature fusion (called "cold fusion") is not available at the present time, fission is used to fuel nuclear power plants. Uranium fuel rods produce heat as their nuclei split apart. Water flows around the rods. This hot water is then used to heat secondary water to produce steam. A wall between the two water sources prevents radiation from entering the secondary water source. The steam is used to move turbines, which then produce electricity. The purpose of the nuclear power plant is not to produce nuclear energy, but to use nuclear energy to produce electricity.

Nuclear energy has many advantages. It is more efficient, using less fuel to produce the same amount of electricity, than other forms of fuel. And other than the radiation produced, there is very little pollution. However, storing spent fuel rods and other contaminated materials is a serious issue for nuclear power plants. These materials remain radioactive for a very long period of time and must be stored where they will not affect people.

Despite the fears that many people have of nuclear energy, it is a very safe energy source. Power plants are built inside concrete containment buildings that prevent the escape of radiation, even in the event of an accident. Nuclear reactors are even used to power submarines and aircraft carriers for the U.S. Navy. ■

WHAT DID WE LEARN?

- What is nuclear power?
- What is nuclear fission?
- What is nuclear fusion?
- Which nuclear process is used in nuclear power plants?

TAKING IT FURTHER

- Why is this process used in nuclear power plants?
- Why are some submarines built with nuclear power plants instead of diesel engines?
- How might nuclear waste be safely stored?

NUCLEAR RADIATION

Nuclear energy depends on materials that are **radioactive**. A material is considered radioactive if it has an unstable nucleus. Some materials only become stable by losing parts of their nucleus and releasing nuclear energy in the form of radiation. Radiation can occur in one of three forms.

A nuclear power plant

The first type of radiation is called alpha radiation. **Alpha particles** consist of two protons and two neutrons—essentially a helium nucleus—that breaks off of the original nucleus. Alpha particles move relatively slowly and can travel about four inches. Alpha particles can be stopped by something as thin as a piece of paper. Because alpha particles are basically helium atoms without electrons, it is believed that much of the helium found in the crust of the earth and in the atmosphere is a result of radioactive materials inside the earth.

The second type of radiation that is released by radioactive materials is called beta radiation. **Beta particles** are high-speed electrons that are released when a neutron is converted into a proton and an electron. A beta particle can travel at nearly the speed of light and can only be stopped by something as thick as a sheet of copper.

The most dangerous type of radiation is the third type— gamma radiation. **Gamma radiation** is released in the form of very powerful electromagnetic waves. These waves of energy travel at the speed of light and can penetrate most materials. A ½-inch (1.3 cm) thick piece of lead will reduce the intensity of the gamma rays by about half. Although gamma radiation in particular can be deadly, there are many positive uses for radiation. Do some research and find at least three positive uses for radiation.

Nuclear Weapons

"The Bomb"

LESSON 5

How does a nuclear bomb work?

Words to know:

atomic bomb

hydrogen bomb

thermonuclear weapon

Challenge words:

radioactive decay

radiometric dating

Nuclear energy is much more powerful than chemical energy. Therefore, it was natural to try to use nuclear energy to produce a more powerful bomb. In fact, a nuclear explosion is thousands or even millions of times more powerful than a chemical explosion like dynamite (TNT). The first nuclear weapons were developed during the Second World War.

Early nuclear weapons, or atomic bombs, were fission-type weapons in which uranium or plutonium nuclei were split to release incredible amounts of power. Nuclear explosions create a fireball and a blast wave with huge amounts of energy. The blast wave from a nuclear explosion can knock down buildings. Nuclear weapons have only been used twice in war. The United States released two nuclear bombs on Japan during World War II.

After the war ended, the fusion bomb was developed. This weapon is also called a hydrogen bomb because the energy is released as hydrogen atoms fuse to form helium atoms. As we mentioned in the previous lesson, fusion can only occur at very high temperatures, like in the sun. Therefore, a small fission reaction is used as a trigger in order to produce these high temperatures. Because a fusion reaction occurs at such high temperatures, these weapons are sometimes referred to as thermonuclear weapons.

The power of a nuclear weapon is often referred to in terms of how many tons of TNT would produce the same size of explosion. Fission reactions are smaller than fusion reactions and are usually said to be equivalent to thousands of tons of TNT. They are called kiloton reactions. Fusion bombs, on the other hand, are equivalent to millions of tons of TNT and are thus said to be megaton weapons.

FORMS OF ENERGY

Complete the "Forms of Energy Word Search" to review the energy terms you have learned.

A 23-kiloton nuclear explosion
at the Nevada Test Site on April 18, 1953

Early testing of nuclear weapons took place in remote areas such as the desert of New Mexico and on several South Pacific islands. However, the possible fallout from the radiation released during a nuclear explosion is hazardous and can be carried far distances by the wind. So all nuclear testing is now done underground to prevent radiation from spreading to populated areas.

Nuclear weapons are a fearsome power. They are a testimony to man's ingenuity as well as to man's cruelty. And because of the destructive power of nuclear weapons, many people also fear nuclear energy in its nonmilitary forms. However, we need to remember that God designed atoms to possess this energy, and we have a responsibility to use it wisely. ■

WHAT DID WE LEARN?

- What are the two types of nuclear weapons that have been developed?
- Why are fusion bombs sometimes called hydrogen bombs?
- Why are fusion bombs sometimes called thermonuclear weapons?
- How are the high temperatures needed for a fusion reaction achieved in a hydrogen bomb?

TAKING IT FURTHER

- What elements are useful in fission bombs?
- Why are nuclear bomb tests conducted underground?

RADIOMETRIC DATING

Radioactive materials are ones whose nuclei are unstable. The process whereby a nucleus releases radioactive particles and energy is called **radioactive decay**.

The nucleus of a radioactive element will change. After it emits alpha and beta particles, it becomes a new element since it has lost some of its protons. The new element may or may not be radioactive. If the new element is not stable, it will again decay and become a different element. This process will continue until a stable nucleus is achieved.

For example, plutonium-242 is radioactive and will emit an alpha particle. The nucleus then has two fewer protons and two fewer neutrons than before so the element is now uranium-238. Uranium-238 is also radioactive and will emit an alpha particle to become thorium-234, which decays to become protactinium-234, and so on.

Some radioactive elements give off alpha particles very easily and quickly decay. Other elements decay at a very slow rate. The length of time it takes for half of a sample to decay from its original element into its stable element is called the half-life of that element. For example, the half-life of radium-221 is 30 seconds. Radium-221 changes very quickly. Uranium-238 on the other hand changes very slowly and has a half-life of about 4.5 billion years.

You may wonder why uranium is useful in nuclear weapons if its half-life is so long. First of all, uranium ore contains not only U-238 but also U-235, which is separated and used in nuclear weapons and reactors. Also, in a nuclear reaction, speeding neutrons constantly bombard the nuclei of the uranium splitting the nuclei quickly (called *fission*), thus releasing their atomic energy. This is a very different process than natural radioactive decay.

A common use of radioactive elements, other than for nuclear weapons and nuclear power, is for **radiometric dating**. Many evolutionary scientists believe that by measuring the ratio of a radioactive "parent" element to the resulting "daughter" element, and knowing the half-life of the element, they can calculate how long the sample has existed, and therefore how old it is. For example, if a rock contains uranium and thorium, a scientist might conclude that the thorium was a result of the decomposition of the uranium and the ratio of the two indicates the age of the rock.

However, there are several problems with this idea. The scientist is making some assumptions that may not be true. What assumptions are being made? First, the scientist is assuming that when the rock was formed it had no thorium at all. This has been proven not to be the case in many instances.

Second, he is assuming that all of the thorium that is now in the rock came from the decay of uranium; however, it could have come from other sources. He is assuming that all the original uranium has either stayed in the rock or decayed into thorium without leaving the sample through any other means. Also, he is assuming that the rate at which uranium decays has been the same for the entire history of the earth. And finally, he is assuming that the conditions on the earth have been somewhat the same for that very long period of time. If any of these assumptions are not correct, the answer could be flawed. And it is likely that many of those assumptions are wrong.

Radiometric dating has been used to test many rock samples with widely varying results. After testing rocks that were formed in a volcanic eruption in 1800, radiometric dating methods yielded 12 different ages varying from 140 million years to 2.96 billion years, when the rocks were actually about 200 years old.

We can trust what the Bible says. The world was created by God only a few thousand years ago. Don't be misled by radiometric dating. For more on the assumptions and methods of radiometric dating, see www.answersingenesis.org/go/dating.

THE MANHATTAN PROJECT

Not everyone knows what the Manhattan Project was, but almost everyone knows about its outcome—the nuclear bomb. The project began in 1942, less than a year after the Empire of Japan attacked America. When the project began, the United States was at war with Japan, Germany, and Italy. Japan had conquered the Philippines and its navy ruled the Pacific. Germany controlled almost all of Europe and much of North Africa. And the United States had not yet recovered from the attack at Pearl Harbor. The outlook was grim.

Three years earlier in 1939, several prominent Jewish scientists, including Albert Einstein, Leo Szilard, and Eugene Wigner, who had all fled Nazi Germany, wrote a joint letter to President Franklin D. Roosevelt telling him of the work going on in Germany on nuclear weapons. At the time, President Roosevelt hoped he could stop this work through sabotage.

Britain and the U.S. did all they could to slow down the Germans, and by February 1943 it looked like they were succeeding. The SOE, an underground unit helped by the British, planted a bomb at a factory in Norway where a nuclear bomb was being developed. As soon as it was rebuilt, 150 American bombers destroyed it again. Two months later, the Norwegian resistance sank a German boat carrying supplies for their nuclear program. All of these events helped to prevent Germany from completing their nuclear weapon.

However, back in 1940, it looked like the Germans might succeed in building a nuclear weapon. The German army had invaded Denmark and pressed Niels Bohr, the world's leading expert in atomic research, into service. German scientists had already worked with uranium, and Germany had made several large advancements toward the development of an atomic bomb. With the capture of Bohr, America feared Germany would be successful in developing a nuclear weapon.

But it was nearly two years later, in 1942, before the United States set up the Manhattan Project under General Leslie Groves. Groves gathered top scientists from several different nationalities. Many were Jewish and had fled from Europe. Niels Bohr continued to do research for Germany until 1943 when the British Secret Service helped him escape to Sweden and then to America where he joined the Manhattan Project. He worked on the project for the next two years and later returned to Denmark.

Little Boy and Fat Man

The leaders of the Manhattan Project set up three sites around the country. The first was in Oak Ridge, Tennessee. At this site, U-235, the highly radioactive fuel needed for a nuclear weapon, was separated from the more common uranium, U-238. The second site was in Hanford, Washington. Their job was to produce plutonium. At that time, all the known plutonium in the world could fit on the head of a pin with room left over. This site had to make enough plutonium for a bomb. The third site was in Los Alamos, New Mexico, at a remote boys' school that was having problems keeping qualified teachers because of the war. Its remote location and the dormitories left by the boys' school made it an ideal place for the development of the atomic bomb. Here the scientists began doing work that had never been done before and no one knew if it was truly possible.

Robert Oppenheimer, born in New York in 1904, was put in charge of making the bomb work. By March 1943, the small mountain town of Los Alamos had become an intellectual boomtown. Top scientists and engineers were pulled in from all over the country and the world to work on this project. In 1942, at the University of Chicago, Enrico Fermi observed the first nuclear reaction. Immediately after Fermi's demonstration, a series of progressively larger nuclear reactors was built.

By 1945, three bombs had been built, one for a test and the other two to use. The first bomb was tested at Alamogordo, New Mexico on July 16, 1945. The two remaining bombs (recreations are pictured above) were different types. One, called Little Boy, was a gun-type weapon, in which a slug of U-235 was projected down a barrel into the center of a second piece of U-235. The second bomb, Fat Man, had a hollow ball of plutonium surrounded by explosives. When the explosives went off, the explosion forced the plutonium together, compressing it and causing a nuclear explosion.

The bombs were ready, but by this time Germany had surrendered, and America had to decide whether to use the new weapon on Japan or not. The decision to drop the bomb on Japan was not decided by one man but by a committee of top advisors who were asked to very carefully study the problem. This work was not taken lightly—all involved knew this new weapon would change the way the world viewed war and the way they viewed Americans. Many of the scientists who had worked on the project signed a letter petitioning Harry S. Truman, the new president, not to use the bomb. They believed there was evidence that Japan would soon lose the war and surrender. However, the committee believed that if the war did not end soon as many as one million more Americans would die. This was not an easy decision.

It was decided that dropping the bomb would ultimately save lives, so it was up to President Truman to decide when and where to use the new weapon. No one knew exactly what the bombs would do when dropped. Robert Oppenheimer told Paul Tibbets, the man in charge of the planes, that the shock wave from the bombs could crush the planes. Deke Parsons, another person on the Manhattan Project, told the plane crew that the shock wave could crack the earth's crust and was so bright that it could cause blindness. Fortunately, none of those predictions came true. On August 6, 1945, the first bomb was dropped on Hiroshima. Japan did not surrender immediately, so the second bomb was dropped on Nagasaki on August 9, 1945. Japan began negotiations to surrender the next day, and announced their surrender on August 14. The war was finally over.

UNIT 2

THERMAL ENERGY

THERMAL ENERGY

Heating things up

LESSON 6

What is thermal energy and how is it measured?

Words to know:

thermal energy

heat

temperature

calorie

Calorie

Challenge words:

thermal capacity

specific heat

We are all familiar with the concept of temperature. If the weather is cold outside you know to put on a heavy coat and gloves before you go out to shovel the snow. But how is temperature related to thermal energy? And what exactly is thermal energy? Let's start by defining thermal energy. Thermal energy is the kinetic energy that an object's atoms or molecules possess. This is also called heat. This energy is directly related to how fast the molecules or atoms are moving.

We often use thermal energy without realizing it. For example, when your hands feel cold, you rub them together to make them feel warmer. What you are really doing is causing the molecules in your hands to move faster as they rub together. This increases their thermal energy, and thus you feel warmer.

As particles gain more energy and move more quickly, the temperature of the object increases. An object that feels hot has particles that are moving more quickly than the particles in an object that feels cold. Hot and cold are qualitative observations. What one person thinks of as hot, another may think of as just warm. So a more accurate method is used to measure heat. This is where temperature comes in. Temperature is a measurement of the average kinetic energy of an object's particles.

Temperature is measured in units called degrees. There are two common scales used for measuring temperature. The Fahrenheit scale is used in the United States for most temperature measurements. On the Fahrenheit scale, water freezes at 32 degrees and boils at 212 degrees at sea level. The Celsius scale is used in most scientific measurements and in most countries around the world. On the Celsius scale, water freezes at 0 degrees and boils at 100 degrees at sea level.

MEASURING TEMPERATURE & THERMAL ENERGY

Complete the "Thermal Energy" worksheet to gain a better understanding of temperature and thermal energy.

Thermal Energy

FUN FACT

A gram of fat contains 9 Calories of thermal energy. A gram of protein and a gram of carbohydrates each contain only 4 Calories. So if you want to eat the same amount of food but have fewer Calories, eat foods low in fat.

Because both heat and temperature are related to the energy and movement of molecules, it is easy to get them confused. You can remember that temperature is a measure of the average kinetic energy the molecules possess. For example, a cup of hot chocolate has a higher temperature than a cup of iced tea because the molecules of the hot chocolate are moving much more quickly than the molecules in the tea.

Heat, on the other hand, is the total amount of kinetic energy that all the molecules of an object contain. Heat is measured in units called calories. A **calorie** is the amount of energy needed to raise one gram of water one degree Celsius. The number of calories in an item indicates the amount of heat it could release.

Calories contained in food are really equal to 1,000 calories and are designated by a capital C. So if you are told that an apple contains 65 Calories, what it really contains is 65,000 calories as defined above. The Calories contained in food are actually stored as chemical energy that has the potential to produce heat/thermal energy.

If I asked you which has more thermal energy, an ice cube or an iceberg, you might guess correctly that the iceberg has more energy because it is bigger. If you have two samples of the same material that are at the same temperature, the larger piece will have more thermal energy than the smaller piece.

But, which do you think has more thermal energy, a cup of hot chocolate or an iceberg? You might guess that the hot chocolate has more thermal energy because it

WHAT DID WE LEARN?

- What is thermal energy?
- What is temperature?
- What is a calorie?
- How are Calories in food related to thermal energy?

TAKING IT FURTHER

- What happens to the speed of an item's molecules as its temperature increases?
- What happens to the temperature of an item if its molecules slow down?
- Which has more thermal energy, a melted Hershey's kiss or a giant snowman?

has a higher temperature. However, you would be wrong. Each individual molecule in the iceberg has less energy than each individual molecule in the hot chocolate, but when you add up all the energy in all the molecules, the iceberg has more total thermal energy because it has so many more molecules than a cup of hot chocolate.

You can remember that temperature describes average kinetic energy and thermal energy/heat describes total kinetic energy in the particles of an object. ∎

SPECIFIC HEAT

If you add the same amount of heat to two different materials, their temperatures may not necessarily increase by the same amount. Different materials have different capacities for storing or absorbing heat. The ability to store or absorb heat is called **thermal capacity** or **specific heat**. Specific heat is a measurement of the heat energy required to raise the temperature of one gram of material by one degree Celsius. By definition, the specific heat of water is 1 calorie/gram. The specific heats of all other substances are compared to that of water.

Many substances have a lower specific heat than water does. This makes water a good substance for conducting heat from one area to another. List three ways that water is used to conduct heat either for heating or cooling purposes.

Purpose: To demonstrate the differences in specific heat

Materials: water, vegetable oil, thermometer, sauce pan, stove, "Specific Heat" worksheet

Procedure:

1. Allow ½ cup of water and ½ cup of vegetable oil to come to room temperature.

2. Measure the temperature of both samples and verify that they are the same. Record your measurements on a copy of the "Specific Heat" worksheet.

3. Pour the water into a saucepan and heat the water over medium heat for two minutes.

4. Measure the temperature again. How much has the temperature of the water increased?

5. Pour out the water and allow the pan to cool to room temperature.

6. Pour the oil into the saucepan and heat the oil over medium heat for two minutes. **Be sure to remove the oil from the heat. Be careful with hot oil. Do not heat it more than 2 minutes.**

7. Measure the temperature of the oil. How much has the temperature of the oil increased? Complete your worksheet.

Conclusion:

You can see that water and oil have different specific heats. God designed different substances to be able to be used in different applications.

Substance	Specific Heat (cal/g °C)
Salt	0.02
Gold	0.03
Copper	0.09
Glass	0.20
Aluminum	0.21
Ethyl alcohol	0.46
Water	1.00
Helium	1.25
Hydrogen	3.45

FAHRENHEIT & CELSIUS

When we think of the thermometer, we think of a tube filled with mercury or alcohol, or of an electronic device that measures temperature. We also think of the scale on the thermometer as being either in degrees Fahrenheit (°F) or degrees Celsius (°C). This is a fairly accurate description of most thermometers today, but this was not always the case. The thermometer that we know today went through many changes to get where it is now.

It is not clear who invented the thermometer. It is believed that the first device for measuring temperature, called a thermoscope, was invented during the time of Galileo, who receives the credit for building it by most people. Galileo's thermoscope used expanding gas to raise and lower a column of water. However, it was a man named Santorio who first added a scale with numbers to the thermoscope, so some people credit him with inventing the thermometer. The device was probably not the work of one man but came about because of the circle of learned men in

Venice that shared ideas. The early thermoscopes were not very accurate but were instrumental in understanding thermal energy.

In 1714 a German inventor named Daniel Gabriel Fahrenheit invented a mercury thermometer. Daniel was born in 1686, and in 1701 he moved to Amsterdam. Looking for a trade, he became interested in building scientific instruments. He traveled throughout Europe, meeting with scientists and other instrument makers before he returned to Amsterdam. One of the men that Daniel Fahrenheit met was Olaus Roemer who had developed an alcohol thermometer. Roemer set the scale for his thermometer so that 0° represented the melting point of an ice/salt combination and 60° was the boiling point of water.

Daniel Fahrenheit took this idea and expanded upon it. Fahrenheit also set the melting point of the ice/salt combination at 0°F, but set the temperature of the human body at 90°F. He constructed the first mercury-in-glass thermometer in 1714, and in 1724 he added this scale to it.

Using his mercury thermometer, Fahrenheit discovered that water and other liquids had set boiling points that varied with a change in atmospheric pressure. Using this scale it was found that water would freeze at around 30°F (later found to be 32°F) and would boil at 212°F at sea level.

Although Americans are most familiar with temperature in degrees Fahrenheit, most scientists now use the Celsius scale. This scale sets 0°C as the freezing point of water and 100°C as the boiling point of water. The Celsius scale was developed by Anders Celsius in 1742. Although Celsius is best known today for his work with thermometers, his real love was astronomy. Celsius was a Swedish astrono-

mer who succeeded his father as a professor of astronomy in 1730 and built Sweden's first observatory in 1741.

In 1733 Celsius published a collection of 316 aurora borealis observations. He also discovered that the aurora borealis had an influence on compass needles. In 1735 he was the only astronomer that went on an expedition to help answer one of the big questions of the day: was the earth flatter at the poles, as Sir Isaac Newton proposed, or was it flatter near the equator, as many French scientists suggested? The scientists in the expedition determined that the earth was flatter at the poles.

Celsius started many projects. However, most of them remained unfinished when he died at the age of 42. Among these projects was a draft of a science fiction novel taking place partly on the star Sirius.

Although mercury and alcohol glass thermometers are still widely used today, digital or electronic thermometers are becoming increasingly popular. Most digital thermometers use a material whose electrical resistance changes with temperature, thus allowing a different amount of current to flow depending on the temperature. This current is changed into a digital display showing the temperature. Digital thermometers can be calibrated to display the temperature in either degrees Fahrenheit or degrees Celsius.

The thermometer may seem like a very simple scientific instrument, but the work of Celsius and Fahrenheit helped to develop our understanding of thermal energy, which has greatly aided in the understanding of the physical properties of all matter.

Anders Celsius

CONDUCTION

Moving heat

LESSON 7

How is heat transferred during conduction?

Words to know:

conduction

thermal equilibrium

thermal conductor

thermal insulator

Challenge words:

heat of fusion

heat of vaporization

Heat, or thermal energy, is the moving of molecules. Thermal energy can be transferred from one item to another in three different ways. Heat is transferred through conduction, convection, and radiation. We will look at each of these methods in separate lessons. In this lesson we will learn about conduction.

Conduction is the transfer of thermal energy by the actual collision of particles between one item and another. Heat flows from a hotter area to a cooler area as the energy from the faster-moving particles is transferred to the slower-moving particles when they collide with each other. The faster-moving particles bump into the slower-moving particles and some of the kinetic energy is transferred. This causes the faster-moving particles to slow down and the slower-moving particles to speed up.

The particles in one object will continue to transfer energy to another object until the average speed of the particles is the same in both objects. Once the average speed of the objects is the same, then the temperature of both objects will be the same. This situation is called thermal equilibrium.

Conduction is happening all around us. Your ice cream begins to melt because heat from the warm air is being transferred to the ice cream when the air molecules bump into the ice cream molecules, thus warming them up. When you heat a pan of water on the stove, heat is transferred from the stove's heating element to the bottom of the pan through conduction, then from the bottom of the pan to the water molecules that are touching the pan. If you look around you, you will find many examples of warm objects coming in contact with cooler objects and transferring heat as their molecules come in contact with each other.

TESTING CONDUCTORS & INSULATORS

Based on your experience, which materials in your kitchen are best for conducting heat? Which are best for insulating from heat?

Purpose: To test the heat conduction of different materials

Materials: five or more containers made from different materials such as metal, plastic, glass; thermometers

Procedure:

1. Line up the containers in what you think is the order from most conducting to least conducting. Label each container in numerical order, with 1 being what you think is the best heat conductor.

2. Heat several cups of water until boiling.

3. Carefully pour ½ cup of hot water into each container. Do not touch the outside of the containers, especially metal containers.

4. Use the "Conduction" worksheet to record the temperature in each container. Measure the temperature in each container every five minutes for twenty minutes. Record the temperature in each container on the worksheet.

5. After you complete your temperature measurements, answer the questions on the worksheet.

Conduction is the primary way that heat is transferred in solid objects. However, some materials conduct heat more easily than others. Silver is the best conductor of heat or the best **thermal conductor**. Other metals are also good heat conductors. Other solids, such as glass and brick, are less conductive. Some materials, such as cotton and wool, are not good conductors at all.

Most gases, particularly gases that are trapped and cannot move freely, are very poor conductors of heat. A material that does not conduct heat well is called a **thermal insulator**. Insulator comes from the Latin word *insula*, which means an island. One good insulator is fiberglass. Fiberglass is a substance with very small glass fibers that trap air between them. A wool sweater is also a good insulator. The wool does not conduct heat well, plus the spaces between the strands of yarn trap air. This also prevents conduction. Double-paned windows, which are two panes of glass with air trapped between them, make a much better insulator than a single pane of glass.

God has designed birds to be able to use the insulating power of air to keep warm. When the weather is cool, birds fluff up their feathers to trap air next to their bodies. Their bodies warm up the air, but then the air cannot move, so the heat stays close to their bodies and helps to keep them warm. ■

FUN FACT

The ceramic used to make the tiles on the underside of the space shuttle is such a good insulator that you could hold a glowing red tile and it would not burn your hands.

Thermal Energy

WHAT DID WE LEARN?

- What is conduction?
- What is thermal equilibrium?
- Which materials are good conductors of heat?

TAKING IT FURTHER

- Give several examples of thermal insulators and how they are used.
- What is the purpose of using insulating materials in various items?

LATENT HEAT

Not all thermal energy that is transferred into a substance raises the temperature of that substance. Some of the energy is used to overcome attractive forces of the molecules. Energy must be added to ice to overcome the attraction that the ice molecules have for each other before the ice can melt. Similarly, before water is turned into steam, enough energy must be added to break the attraction that the water molecules have for each other. The energy needed to melt a substance is called the latent **heat of fusion**. The energy needed to change a liquid into a gas is called the latent **heat of vaporization**. The heat of fusion and the heat of vaporization are different for each substance.

Purpose: To observe the heat of fusion and the heat of vaporization for water

Materials: ice cubes, saucepan, stove, thermometer, "Heat of Fusion and Vaporization" worksheet

Procedure:

1. Place 1 cup of ice cubes in a saucepan.

2. Heat the ice cubes on medium-low heat, continually stirring the ice/water mixture with a spoon. Hold a thermometer in the water and make sure it is not touching the bottom of the pan when you take measurements.

3. Measure the temperature of the water in the pan every minute and record your measurements on the "Heat of Fusion and Vaporization" worksheet.

4. Continue recording the temperature every minute until the water begins to boil or until you have at least 3 nearly identical readings. Graph your data on the graph paper on the worksheet. Compare your data to the graph below.

Your graph will not have the part of the line that rises after the boiling point, because you will not be able to add energy to the steam after it has left the pan.

Conclusion: You should observe that the temperature of the ice/water mixture stays very close to 0ºC (32ºF) for several minutes before starting to rise. This is because the heat energy from the stove is being used to melt the ice—to change phases from a solid into a liquid. After most of the ice has melted, the temperature of the water will begin to rise quickly. As the water approaches 100ºC (212ºF), the temperature of the water will again stop rising as the energy is used to change phase again—from a liquid into a gas.

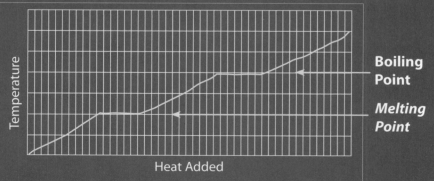

CONVECTION

Currents

LESSON

8

How is heat transferred during convection?

Words to know:

convection

Conduction, the transferring of heat through colliding particles, is only one way that heat is transferred. If we relied on conduction alone to heat a pan of water, it would take a very long time for the water to come to a boil. However, we do not have to rely on conduction alone. Convection aids in the heating of a pan of water, as well as in most other heat transfers.

Convection is the movement of heat through currents. Because gravity pulls down on everything on earth, things that are less dense rise above things that are more dense. The molecules in hot air are moving faster than the molecules in cold air, so the molecules are farther apart and the hot air is less dense than the cooler air. This causes the hot air to rise above the cooler air, and the cooler air to replace the warm air. The same thing is true for water molecules.

In a pan of water heating on the stove, the molecules closest to the stove become warmer through conduction. These molecules are now moving faster than the cooler ones above them. Because they are less dense they begin to rise and the cooler ones take their place. The cooler molecules can now be heated through conduction. This sets up a current of water within the pan allowing the cooler molecules to constantly be replacing the warmer molecules; thus the water heats much more quickly.

In the last lesson, we said that air that is confined (such as in a double-paned window) is a good

OBSERVING CONVECTION

Purpose: To observe convection

Materials: container, cup, blue and red food coloring, water

Procedure:

1. Fill a clear container with very warm water.

2. In a cup, add a few drops of blue food coloring to a small amount of very cold water.

3. Slowly pour the blue/cold water into the warm water. Watch as the blue spreads through the water. Where did the blue water go first?

4. Repeat the experiment, only this time fill the container with very cold water.

5. Add a few drops of red food coloring to a small amount of very warm water in a cup.

6. Slowly pour the red/warm water into the cold water. How is the current generated by the warm water different from the previous experiment?

Conclusion: Warm water is less dense than cold water, so you are observing convection currents as you watch the colored water move throughout the clear water.

insulator. However, air that is free to move actually helps transfer heat because of convection currents that occur in the moving air.

God is the ultimate designer of convection currents. Without convection we would not have the weather systems that bring the needed rain to various parts of the world. Convection on the earth starts with the sun. The sun heats the air near the equator more than it heats the air near the poles. This warm air rises and cooler air takes its place. This sets up convection currents in the atmosphere that move the air around the world. This allows the temperature on the earth to be more moderate. It brings cooler temperatures to the equatorial areas and warmer temperatures to the poles. Convection does not completely mix all of the air around the world, but it does help equalize the temperatures.

Convection also causes the wind to blow. For example, because land is a better conductor of heat than water, the land changes temperature faster than the water. Therefore, when the sun rises in the morning the land heats faster than the ocean. The air over the land therefore heats faster than the air over the ocean. This warm air rises and cooler air from over the water takes its place. Thus, a breeze comes from the

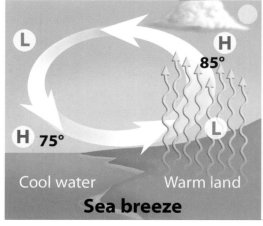

Cool water   Warm land
Sea breeze

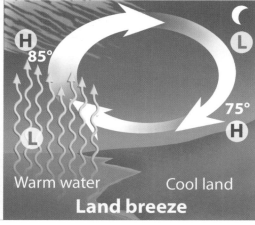

Warm water   Cool land
Land breeze

water toward the land. This is called a sea breeze. During the day, the land and the sea have about the same temperature so there is little breeze. But after the sun sets, the land cools more quickly than the ocean so the air above the water becomes less dense than the air above the land. Thus, the air moves from the land toward the water. This is called a land breeze. Convection is God's way of providing the needed air currents and winds for our weather.

Man has also learned to use convection. Not only is convection important in heating water on the stove, convection ovens also move the air in currents to help food cook more quickly and evenly. Hot water and forced-air heating systems both rely on air currents to move the warm air around a room. And convection is important in moving water through the radiator of your car to help keep your engine from overheating. ■

WHAT DID WE LEARN?

- What is convection?
- What causes convection?
- How does convection affect the weather on earth?

TAKING IT FURTHER

- Why does convection allow materials to heat or cool faster?
- Ideally, where would you place heating vents to most efficiently warm a house?
- Ideally, where would you place air conditioning vents to most efficiently cool a house?

APPLIANCE DESIGN

Using what you know about conduction and convection, design a refrigerator and a stove. Show where you would place the cooling and/or heating coils. Also, show how you would use insulating and conducting materials.

RADIATION

Don't get sunburned!

LESSON 9

How is heat transferred during radiation?

Words to know:

thermal radiation

infrared radiation

Convection and conduction both transfer heat through the movement of molecules. However, we know that the sun heats the earth, yet there are virtually no molecules in outer space between the sun and the earth. So how does heat from the sun reach the earth? There is another method for transferring heat. Scientists call it radiation.

Thermal radiation is the transfer of thermal energy by electromagnetic waves. Light rays are one type of electromagnetic waves. When light rays hit an object, some of the energy is converted into heat. This is especially true for infrared wavelengths of light. Much of the energy from the sun is in the form of infrared radiation. It is believed that all electromagnetic waves can be converted into heat, but infrared radiation is most easily converted and causes the most increase in temperature.

We experience radiated heat in many ways. You feel warmer standing in the sunshine than in the shadows because the radiated heat can reach your skin. Your car also heats up on a sunny day because the radiated energy passes through the glass, turns to heat when it hits the seats, and then becomes trapped inside the car. This is the same effect that nurseries use to keep greenhouses warm in the winter. In fact, this is called the *greenhouse effect*.

The greenhouse effect makes a greenhouse warm.

TESTING FOR RADIATED ENERGY

Purpose: To see the effects of color on radiation absorption

Materials: two cups, black paper, white paper, thermometer

Procedure:

1. Cover the outside of one cup with black paper and cover a second cup with white paper.

2. Fill both cups with the same amount of water and measure the temperature of the water in each cup. The temperature should be the same.

3. Place both cups in a sunny location.

4. Predict what will happen to the temperature of the water in each cup and write your hypothesis on a sheet of paper.

5. Measure the temperature of the water every five minutes for 20 minutes, and write your measurements on the paper.

6. At the end of 20 minutes, compare the temperature of the water in each cup.

Questions:

- How does the temperature of the water in each cup compare?

- Which water heated up the most?

- Did this match your hypothesis?

- Why is the water in the cup covered in black paper warmer than the water in the cup with white paper?

Different kinds of matter absorb different amounts of radiated energy. Also, different colors absorb different amounts of radiated energy. Darker colors, particularly black, absorb more heat. Lighter colors, especially white, reflect most of the light and radiation. This is why people tend to wear lighter colors in the summer and darker colors in the winter. The light-colored clothing reflects most of the radiated energy and thus helps to keep you cool. Darker clothing absorbs more of the radiated heat and helps to keep you warm. Radiated heat is absorbed by black asphalt and dark dirt more than by grass, so when snow begins falling it will melt on the streets but begin collecting on the grass. And in the summer, you would rather lie on the grass than on the sidewalk, because the radiated heat makes the sidewalk too hot. ■

FUN FACT

In Antarctica, 90% of all thermal radiation is reflected by the white snow and ice, so very little of it is turned into heat. This keeps the area cool and prevents much of the snow and ice from melting.

Asphalt absorbs and radiates heat because it is a dark color.

WHAT DID WE LEARN?

- What is thermal radiation?
- Which type of electromagnetic waves most easily transfer heat energy?
- Which colors best absorb radiated heat?

TAKING IT FURTHER

- Why do we know that heat is not transferred from the sun by conduction or convection?
- What color are the seats in most cars? Why are they these colors?
- Why do many people in hot climates wear dark-colored robes?

UNDERSTANDING A THERMOS

To the right is a diagram of the inside of a thermos. Use what you have learned about conduction, convection, and thermal radiation to explain how each part of the thermos works to keep the temperature inside the thermos from changing. Write your ideas on a copy of "Understanding a Thermos" worksheet.

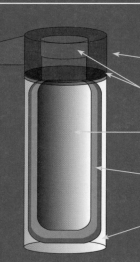

Lids can be sealed tight

Two lids with dead air space between

Inside of bottle covered with mirror coating

A vacuum between two glass layers

Outer plastic shell does not touch inner glass layers

SOLAR & GEOTHERMAL ENERGY

Natural heat

LESSON 10

How can we get and use energy from the sun and earth?

Words to know:

solar energy

geothermal energy

Electricity is the most useful form of energy today. However, heat plays an integral part in bringing electricity to our homes and offices. Power plants use electromagnets to generate electricity. Steam is used to turn the turbines in these magnets, and heat is needed to turn water into steam. Therefore, the vast majority of the power plants need heat to generate electricity.

We have already seen that nuclear reactions generate heat that can be used in power plants. Also, fossil fuels—primarily coal and oil—are burned in many power plants. But God has given us a couple of natural sources of heat that can also be used in power plants. We learned in the last lesson that radiation from the sun generates heat. This is **solar energy**. This radiation can be used in several ways. First, solar panels are boxes with water pipes going through them. The boxes are black on the inside and covered with glass to trap the radiated heat. This heat is transferred to the water as it flows through the pipes. Most solar panels are used in homes to heat water for showers and washing and to heat the building. A few power plants use

solar energy to heat water, but because the sun's rays are spread out, it is necessary to concentrate the rays to produce enough heat for a power plant. This is usually not cost effective; however, research is being done to try to improve the effectiveness of solar energy.

Another natural source of heat is **geothermal energy**. Geothermal means heat from the earth. Most scientists believe that the center of the earth is

Old Faithful geyser
at Yellowstone National Park

extremely hot, perhaps as hot as the surface of the sun. This heat melts the surrounding rock, turning it into magma. Some heat from the center of the earth reaches the surface or nearly to the surface, where it can be accessed for our energy needs. We see evidence of this heat in areas such as Yellowstone National Park where mud pots bubble up, and geysers regularly erupt because of the underground heat.

Most of the geothermal energy is too deep within the earth to be reached. However, power plants have been built in several areas where the heat reaches close to the surface. Most geothermal power plants are located in Iceland, New Zealand, Japan, and China. A few geothermal plants are in Europe, Africa, and the United States. Geothermal energy is most easily accessed near a break between tectonic plates.

To access geothermal energy, a well must be drilled into the rock. These wells are usually 1,000 to 10,000 feet (300–3,000 m) deep. Heated water from these wells is pumped up and used to produce steam in the power plant. If a well does not naturally have water in it, two wells

UNDERSTANDING GEOTHERMAL ENERGY

Geothermal power plants obtain heat by using water that is heated by the rocks inside the earth.

Purpose: To demonstrate how geothermal energy works

Materials: baking pan, rocks, oven, cup, thermometer, colander, large bowl

Procedure:

1. Place 15–20 rocks that are 2–3 inches in diameter in a baking pan.

2. Heat the rocks in an oven at 200˚F for 20 minutes.

3. While the rocks are heating, fill a cup with tap water. Use a thermometer to measure the temperature of the water.

4. Place a colander over a large bowl or pot.

5. When the rocks are warm, use baking mitts to carefully move the rocks into the colander, stacking them closely together.

6. Slowly pour the water over the rocks.

7. Remove the colander and measure the temperature of the water.

Conclusion: The temperature should be several degrees higher. The rocks inside the earth's crust are many times hotter than your rocks, and the heat cannot easily escape into the air, so the water in the earth is heated to a much higher temperature. In fact, because the water is often under pressure, underground water can become super-heated. That is, it becomes hotter than the boiling point of water without turning to steam. When the water is depressurized, it quickly turns to steam and is useful for turning turbines in a power plant.

FUN FACT

You may have seen a calculator that does not need batteries. It usually has a silver panel that provides the necessary power when light is present. This is a photovoltaic or photoelectric panel. These panels are designed to convert light energy directly into electricity. Photoelectric cells are being used for many applications, but they are not yet efficient enough to use on a large scale such as in a power plant. Sunlight is fairly spread out, so it needs to be concentrated to make it efficient to produce electricity. With more research, we may someday be able to use sunlight to produce electricity on a larger scale.

will be drilled. Water is poured down into the first well. It then flows through hot rocks below the surface into the second well. The heated water is then pumped up and used. As it cools, the water is then returned to the first well and recycled to be heated again.

Solar energy and geothermal energy are both considered renewable energy sources because they cannot easily be used up. For all practical purposes, they are infinite. In reality, the heat from the sun or the center of the earth could eventually be used up; however, the length of time for that to occur is millions of years, so there is not much concern about them running out. More research is being conducted into ways to better use these natural sources of heat energy. ■

WHAT DID WE LEARN?

- What is solar energy?
- What is geothermal energy?
- How is solar energy used?
- How is geothermal energy used?

TAKING IT FURTHER

- Why is it difficult to build geothermal power plants in most areas?
- Why are geothermal and solar energy being investigated?
- Why is heat necessary for most electricity?

SOLAR OVEN

Design a solar oven that can harness the heat of the sun to heat your food. Think about what kind of surfaces reflect and absorb solar energy and how you might concentrate the sun's energy. Also, think about ways to prevent heat from conducting away from your oven. Build a solar oven and try it out. (See the Answer Key in the Teacher Supplement if you need some ideas or search the Internet for "solar cooker.")

UNIT 3

ELECTRICITY

ELECTRICITY

Lighting up your world

LESSON
11

What causes electricity?

Words to know:

electron

proton

neutron

ion

law of charges

static electricity

valence electrons

Electricity is the source of energy for most modern conveniences. Nearly everything in your home is powered by electricity. Your refrigerator, your TV, your lights, and your garage-door opener all need electricity to work. Electricity is vital to the modern way of life. But do you really know what electricity is, other than something that comes out of a socket in the wall? Let's take a look at this wonderful source of energy.

Everything in the world is made of tiny particles called atoms. Atoms contain three different parts: electrons, protons, and neutrons. Electrons have a negative electrical charge, protons have a positive electrical charge, and neutrons are neutral, or have no charge. In general, atoms have the same number of electrons and protons, causing them to be electrically neutral. However, if one or more electrons are transferred from one atom to another, electrically-charged particles called ions are formed.

Electricity is the movement of electrons. Because atoms desire to be electrically neutral, oppositely-charged particles are attracted to each other, and similarly-charged particles repel each other. This is the law of charges. And this is the force behind electricity. This attraction and repulsion is what makes electrons move.

Static electricity is a stationary electrical charge. You have probably experienced static elec-

FUN FACT

The word electricity comes from the Greek word *elektron*. This word means amber. Amber is fossilized tree resin and it is a material that easily holds an electrical charge.

FUN WITH STATIC ELECTRICITY

Purpose: To experiment with static electricity

Materials: balloon

Procedure:

1. Blow up a balloon and tie it shut. Try to stick the balloon to the ceiling or wall. Did it stay?

2. Now rub the balloon against your hair several times. Again, try to stick the balloon to the ceiling or wall. Did it stay?

Questions:

• Why does the balloon stick to the ceiling or wall after rubbing it against your hair?

• How did your hair look after rubbing it with the balloon?

• Why did your hair stick out?

• See how long the balloon will stick to the ceiling or wall. Why does it eventually fall off?

Electricity

tricity. Sometime you have walked across the rug and then touched a light switch and been greeted with an unpleasant shock. This happens when friction between your shoes and the carpet removes some electrons from the carpet. These electrons build up on your body so you now have a negative charge with respect to most things around you. When you touch the light switch, the excess electrons are quickly able to flow away from your body and you experience a shock.

Valence electrons are the outermost electrons in an atom. When valence electrons are moved from one place to another, like from the carpet to your body, that item will build up a static electrical charge. It is called static electricity because once the electrons move, they stay where they are until they reach a conductor. Some items give up their electrons more easily than others. How easily atoms give up their electrons determines how well they conduct electricity. The air does not conduct electricity very well, so when your body has excess electrons, they do not transfer into the air. You must touch something that easily conducts electricity, like the metal screws on a light switch cover, before the excess electrons will flow away from your body. ■

FUN FACT

The human nervous system works by passing electrical signals from one nerve to another. The flow of electrons throughout the human body allows us to see, hear, smell, taste, and feel the world around us.

WHAT DID WE LEARN?

• What is electricity?

• What is static electricity?

• What is the law of charges?

TAKING IT FURTHER

• Give other examples of static electricity that you have experienced.

USES FOR STATIC ELECTRICITY

Static electricity is important in the design of many copiers and printers. In a laser printer or copier, a laser is used to generate tiny spots of static electricity on the paper. The toner is attracted to these charged areas. Then the toner is pressed onto the paper and creates a copy.

Another positive use for static electricity is in reducing pollution. Many processes generate smoke—air that contains small particles. Explain how static electricity could be used to eliminate these particles from the air before it is released into the atmosphere.

Although static electricity has some uses, the sudden discharge of static electricity can have damaging effects on many pieces of electrical equipment. Often people use a surge protector with their computers to prevent a sudden surge of electricity from damaging the computers. Design a way to protect yourself from static electricity shocks.

FUN FACT

The lightning bolt is a dramatic example of static electricity in action. You see lightning when a spark of moving electrons races up or down between a cloud and the ground (or between two clouds).

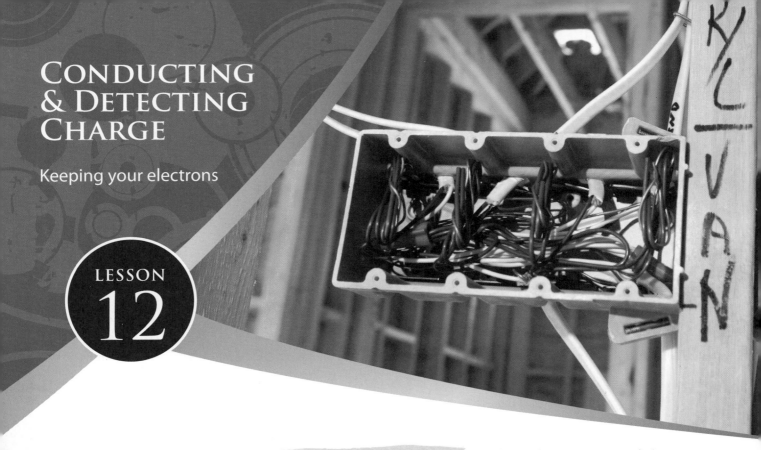

CONDUCTING & DETECTING CHARGE

Keeping your electrons

LESSON 12

How is electricity controlled?

Words to know:

electrical conductor

electrical insulator

semiconductor

Challenge words:

integrated circuit

transistor

Electricity is the flow of electrons. Without the movement of electrons, there would be no electricity. But in order for electricity to be useful, we must be able to control the flow of electrons. God knew this and created some materials that allow electrons to flow easily and other materials that do not allow electrons to flow easily. Materials that allow electrons to flow easily are called **electrical conductors**. These are materials that loosely hold on to their valence electrons, which are the outermost electrons in the atom. Conductors are elements located in the left half of the periodic table. Most metals are very good conductors of electricity. Interestingly, the movement of electrons is also related to the conduction of heat. So in general, materials that conduct electricity also conduct heat well.

Just as materials that do not conduct heat well are called thermal insulators, so materials that do not conduct electricity well are called **electrical insulators**. Insulating elements are found on the far right side of the periodic table. Some common electrical insulators that are not elements, and thus not on the periodic table, include wood, plastic, and rubber.

In a diagonal line on the periodic table from boron to astatine, are a few elements that are neither conductors nor insulators. These elements allow small amounts of electricity to flow through them. They are called **semiconductors**. Semiconductors play an important role in modern technology. Because they allow small amounts of electricity to flow, they can move electrons quickly without generating or conducting large amounts of heat. This has allowed for the development of integrated circuits and thus the development of computers, cell phones, and many other modern electronic devices.

The use of electricity did not start with semiconductors, however. Early

MAKING AN ELECTROSCOPE

Electricity is invisible. We can't see electrons flowing through something. So how do we know if something is electrically charged? We can see the effects of the electricity. For example, your hair stuck out when you rubbed it with a balloon. Sometimes you can see a spark when you get a shock from static electricity. But to detect smaller charges, it is necessary to have a more sensitive charge detector.

Purpose: To build a charge detector called an electroscope

Materials: aluminum foil, paper clip, small jar, modeling clay, plastic comb, balloon

Procedure:

1. Cut a piece of aluminum foil 2 inches long by ¾ inch wide and fold it in half.

2. Straighten a paper clip so that it makes an L.

3. Place the foil over the part of the paper clip that is sticking out and set it inside a small jar.

4. Form a piece of modeling clay into a lid for the jar.

5. Stick the long part of the paper clip through the clay so that the foil hangs in the center of the jar with part of the paper clip sticking out of the clay at the top. You now have an electroscope.

6. Now you can test your electroscope. Comb your hair several times with a plastic comb. Hold the comb near the top of the paper clip.

Questions:

• What happened to the foil? Why do the ends move outward?

• Try this with a balloon instead of a comb. Are the results the same?

• Try generating a charge using other insulating and conducting materials. Which materials produced a detectable charge?

scientists generated charges by rubbing different materials together. They found that they were able to generate the most charge by rubbing two different insulators together. This charge was then stored in a device to be used at a later time. The first storage device was a special jar designed by a scientist named Leyden. The Leyden jar (shown at right) was invented in 1746. It was a glass jar that was coated inside and out with tin or lead. The lid contained a metal bar connected to a chain inside the jar. A charged object was placed near the bar and the electrons moved from the charged object into the jar. The charge stayed inside the jar because of the insulating layer of glass. Eventually better devices were developed for storing charge. Today we use devices called capacitors to store charge. ■

Leyden jar

Electroscope

Electricity

WHAT DID WE LEARN?

- What is an electrical conductor?
- What is an electrical insulator?
- What is a semiconductor?
- What materials are good conductors of electricity?
- What materials are good electrical insulators?

TAKING IT FURTHER

- If a material is a good conductor of heat, is it likely to be an electrical conductor or an electrical insulator?
- Ceramic is an insulator for heat. How well would you expect it to conduct electricity?
- Neon is an element in the far right column of the periodic table. Would you expect it to be an electrical conductor or an insulator?

INTEGRATED CIRCUITS

Integrated circuits are a very important application of electricity in today's society. Nearly every electronic device contains at least one integrated circuit (IC). ICs are made from a special material called a semiconductor. Silicon is the most common semiconductor used today.

To begin with, a cylinder of silicon is sliced into thin wafers. Then tiny **transistors**, which serve as switches, are formed in the silicon, resulting in a series of rectangular circuits like the ones shown here. There are millions of switches in a single IC. These switches allow electrons to flow along specific paths under certain conditions.

In digital circuits, the electricity is generated in pulses. The transistors direct these pulses through different parts of the circuit to achieve specific results using logic "gates." There are essentially three types of gates. The first gate is called an "or" gate, and is shown by this symbol: ⫣⊃

The lines on the left indicate the inputs to the gate and the line on the right is the output of the gate. In an "or" gate, if either of the inputs is on—conducting electricity—then the output will conduct electricity. To make it easy to see what is going on, we say that if a line is conducting electricity it is a 1 and if it is not conducting electricity it is a 0. So if either input to an "or" gate is a 1, the output is a 1, and the "gate" is opened to allow the signal through.

A second kind of logic gate is an "and" gate denoted by the ⫣⊃ symbol. In an "and" gate, the output will be a 1 only if both of the inputs are 1. The third logic

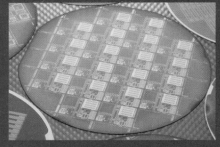

symbol is an inverter. An inverter changes the output to be the opposite of the input, so if the input is a 1 the output will be a 0 and if the input is a 0 the output will be a 1. An inverter is denoted by this symbol: ⊳∘

Complete the "Integrated Circuits" worksheet to demonstrate your understanding of ICs.

1. 0 0 ⟩— 1 0 ⟩— 0 1 ⟩— 1 1 ⟩—

2. 0 0 ⊐— 1 0 [B]— 0 1 [C]— 1 1 [D]

3. 1 ⊳∘— 0 ⊳∘—

LIGHTNING

And thunder

LESSON
13

What causes lightning?

Words to know:

lightning

thunder

Benjamin Franklin is well known for his famous lightning experiment. Most people picture Mr. Franklin standing in the rain, flying a kite up into a thunderstorm and holding onto a metal key to see if he would get shocked. This, of course, is not how it happened. In 1752, Ben Franklin did fly a kite in a thunderstorm. And he did have a key attached by a silk cord to the wet kite string. However, Ben himself was in a shelter, and he did not touch the key. Instead, he held objects close to the key to see if a spark would jump from the key. He found that when he held a charged Leyden jar next to the key a spark did indeed jump from the key to the jar, thus showing that the lightning storm generated electricity.

Sometime later, Ben Franklin invented a way to protect buildings from being struck by lightning. He invented the lightning rod. A lightning rod is a metal rod attached to the top of a building. The rod has a wire attached to it that goes into the ground. If the rod is struck by lightning, the electricity is conducted down the wire into the ground, thus protecting the building.

Today we better understand the causes and effects of lightning. Lightning begins with friction. As water drops, ice crystals, and hail are

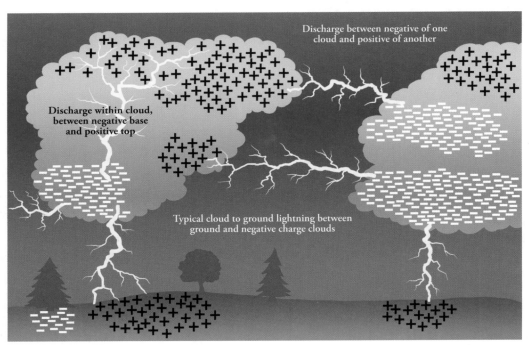

Lightning occurs when positive and negative imbalances create discharges.

moving around inside a thundercloud they bump against one another and against the rising air molecules. This sometimes causes the water and hail to break into smaller charged particles. The positively-charged particles build up in the tops of the clouds and negatively-charged particles build up in the bottoms of the clouds. The air acts as an insulator between these charged areas.

As the charge continues to build up, eventually the

FUN FACT

Lightning strikes somewhere on the earth about 100 times per second.

 # LIGHTNING IN YOUR MOUTH

Purpose: To create electrical charges in your mouth

Materials: Wint-O-Green or Pep-O-Mint Life Saver candies, dark room, mirror

Procedure:

1. Go to a really dark room and stand in front of the mirror. Wait a few minutes until your eyes get accustomed to the darkness.

2. Put a Wint-O-Green or a Pep-O-Mint Life Saver in your mouth.

3. While keeping your mouth open, break the lifesaver up with your teeth and look for sparks. If you do it right, you should see bluish flashes of light.

Conclusion:

Why does this happen? The effect is called triboluminescence, which is similar to the electrical charge build-up that produces lightning, only much less spectacular. When you break the Life Saver apart, you're breaking apart the sugars inside the candy, forcing some electrons out of their atomic fields. These free electrons bump into nitrogen molecules in the air. When they collide, the electrons impart energy to the nitrogen molecules, causing them to vibrate. In this excited state, and in order to get rid of the excess energy, these nitrogen molecules emit light.

attraction between the differing charges becomes greater than the insulating power of the air, and there is a quick discharge of electricity as the electrons rapidly move to an area of opposite charge. This discharge can occur within the cloud, between one cloud and another cloud, or between the cloud and the ground. This discharge of electricity is what we call lightning.

Lightning releases an enormous amount of energy in the form of light and heat. The heat released warms the air molecules around the lightning bolt. This causes the air to expand and then contract very quickly. The rapidly expanding air can cause a sonic boom, which means that the air is moving faster than the speed of sound. This is the sound that we recognize as **thunder**. ■

Many tall buildings have lightning rods.

Electricity

WHAT DID WE LEARN?

- What is lightning?
- What causes lightning?
- What is thunder?
- What causes the air molecules to move quickly enough to generate thunder?

TAKING IT FURTHER

- Why do thunderstorms with lightning occur most often on hot summer days?

NITROGEN CYCLE

Research the nitrogen cycle. Write a paragraph explaining lightning's role in plant growth.

Lightning helps nitrates return to the soil. What other ways can nitrates enter the soil?

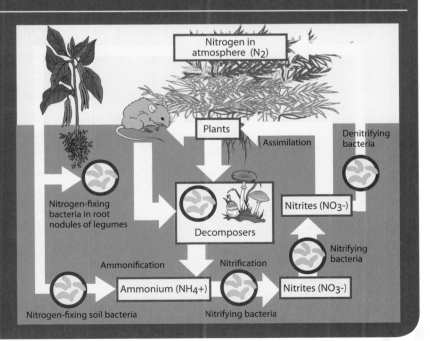

Nitrogen in atmosphere (N_2)

Plants

Assimilation

Denitrifying bacteria

Nitrogen-fixing bacteria in root nodules of legumes

Decomposers

Nitrites (NO_3-)

Nitrifying bacteria

Ammonification

Nitrification

Nitrogen-fixing soil bacteria

Ammonium (NH_4+)

Nitrifying bacteria

Nitrites (NO_3-)

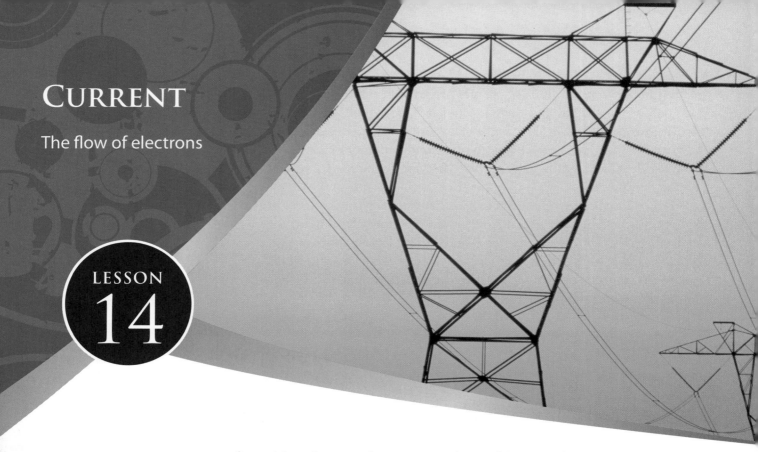

CURRENT

The flow of electrons

How does electricity flow?

Words to know:

current

circuit

battery

switch

Although static electricity can be useful, most electrical devices in use today require a flow of electrons. This flow is called current. Current must flow in a circular path called a circuit. The current in a circuit can be supplied in many different ways. One common source of current is a battery.

A battery is a device that produces electricity by a chemical reaction. As long as the reaction continues, and the circuit is complete, electrons are supplied and the current will flow. When one of the chemicals in the battery is used up, the battery can no longer supply electrons, and we say that the battery is dead. Batteries are used in many electronic devices. From CD players to video games, batteries supply electricity for entertainment. Batteries are also used to provide the electricity needed to start your car. Electric cars even use batteries to supply most or all of the energy needed to make the car move.

Not all current comes from batteries. Much of the electricity we use today is supplied to our houses and other buildings by power plants and can be accessed through the outlets in our walls. Current flows into the device through one side of the outlet and back out through the other side making a complete circuit with the power plant.

Current will continue to flow as long as there is a complete path for it to follow. Sometimes a break can occur in the circuit. This will stop the flow of electrons.

FUN FACT

Rechargeable batteries can be recharged by forcing current to flow in the opposite direction, thus reversing the chemical reaction. This restores the original chemicals, allowing the original reaction to resume when charging is complete.

UNDERSTANDING CIRCUITS

When you turn on a flashlight, you are completing a circuit, which allows current to flow out of the batteries, through the light bulb, and back to the batteries. Below is a diagram showing the circuit in a flashlight. Turn your flashlight on and off. Now open the flashlight and look at the switch mechanism. See if you can determine how it connects and disconnects the batteries to the bulb. Some flashlights have a sliding switch or push button that pushes the wire up against a metal plate that is connected to the light bulb. Other flashlights twist on and off. When the flashlight is off, an air gap exists between the circuitry.

Purpose: To test various materials as conductors

Materials: flashlight, batteries, tag board, foil or coin, tape

Procedure:

1. Cut a small piece of tag board and place it between the batteries in your flashlight. If your flashlight has only one battery, place the cardboard in the bottom of the flashlight.

2. Reassemble your flashlight and try to turn it on. Does it work? Why won't the light come on?

3. Remove the tag board and place a metal coin (or a piece of foil) between the batteries.

4. Reassemble the flashlight and try to turn it on. Does it work? Why does it work?

5. Remove the coin and place plastic tape across one end of one of your batteries.

6. Again, reassemble and try your flashlight. Does it work? Why not?

7. Remove the tape and reassemble your flashlight. It should work again because the circuit is restored.

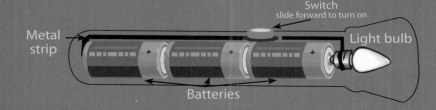

Metal strip · Switch slide forward to turn on · Light bulb · Batteries

This can be very inconvenient such as when a filament inside a light bulb burns up and the light goes out or if someone accidentally cuts through a power line and you lose electricity. Sometimes a problem occurs when a short circuit develops. Electrical devices have a cord with two wires. Each wire is surrounded by insulating material that keeps the wires apart and allows current to flow in opposite directions in each wire. If the insulation breaks down or is cut, the wires may touch. This allows the current to flow directly from one wire into the other, bypassing the device that you are trying to power. The current has found a shorter path or a shorter circuit, thus the name "short circuit." When any of these conditions exist, the intended path must be restored before you can use the device again.

Not all breaks in a circuit are unintentional. Sometimes, a circuit is designed to have a switch that can open or close the circuit at desired times. A light switch allows us to connect and disconnect the wire going to the light bulb, thus allowing us to turn the light on and off easily. Most devices are designed with some kind of switch to control the flow of electrons through the device. ■

WHAT DID WE LEARN?

- What is current?
- Name two ways to generate current.
- What is a circuit?
- What is a short circuit?

TAKING IT FURTHER

- Why is current more useful in many situations than static electricity?
- Some flashlights are waterproof. Why is it important to keep water out of a flashlight?

CIRCUIT GAME

Have you ever played the game "Operation" where you try to remove the patient's funny bone without touching the sides of the hole with your tweezers and setting off the buzzer? This game works on the principle of a complete circuit allowing current to flow. When the tweezers touch the metal of the hole, the circuit is complete and current flows to the buzzer. In a similar way, you can make a fun skills test.

Purpose: To make a skill test using an electrical circuit

Materials: three copper wires, battery, flashlight bulb

Procedure:

1. Tape a long copper wire to one end of a battery.

2. Strip the insulation off of the wire and bend it in funny ways, similar to the picture shown here.

3. Tape a second wire to the other end of the battery and to the bottom of a flashlight bulb. This wire only needs to be stripped on the ends.

4. Tape a third wire to the side of the light bulb and form a loop

in the other end of the wire. The smaller you make the loop, the harder the game will be.

5. Slip the loop over the end of the first wire, and try to move the loop along the twists and turns without touching the wire. If you touch the wire, the circuit will be complete, the bulb will light up, and you lose. Who can move the loop the farthest without making the bulb light up?

MICHAEL FARADAY

1791–1867

Michael Faraday was a man with only an elementary education who became one of the greatest experimenters ever, as well as a strong Christian leader. Michael Faraday was born to a blacksmith on September 22, 1791, in an area that is now part of London. His father had poor health and the family moved frequently as he tried to find steady work. This made life difficult for the Faraday family, but the family was able to stay close because of their strong faith in God. This faith had a great influence on Michael Faraday throughout his life.

When Michael was thirteen years old he started his first job to help the family out. At fourteen, he was taken on as an apprentice bookbinder. While he worked for the bookbinder, which he did in "proper manner," he spent his free time reading the books that he helped produce. He enjoyed the scientific books the most.

In 1810, Michael started attending science lectures, and in 1812, he attended and took extensive notes on lectures by Humphry Davy at the British Royal Institution. At the end of 1812, Faraday sent a copy of his notes to Humphry Davy seeking a position in his lab. Davy agreed to meet with Faraday and advised him to keep working as a bookbinder. However, when an opening came up in the British Royal Institution lab under Davy, he sent for Michael Faraday who took the position. Three years after joining the lab, Michael published his first paper. While under Humphry Davy, he went with Davy on a lecture tour around Europe. The passports they used were given to them by Napoleon.

The year 1821 was one of the most important in Michael Faraday's life. He became the Superintendent of the House at the British Royal Institution, he married Sarah Barnard, the daughter of a leading family in his church, and he made his first major contribution to natural science when he discovered electromagnetic rotation—the principle behind electric motors. Over the next several years, Faraday made many more advancements in science including the understanding of generators, which today provide the majority of the electricity for our society.

Michael Faraday did many experiments in electrochemistry and electromagnetism. Many consider him to be one of the greatest experimenters of all time. But more importantly, those who really knew him considered him a strong Christian. Even while under a heavy schedule in the lab, Michael Faraday was very dedicated to attending his all-day Sunday church service and his midweek service. He studied God's Word with the same intensity he studied science. After his death, it was discovered that his Bible had almost 3,000 notes in the margin! He viewed science as a constant search for truth about God's creation.

VOLTAGE & POWER

Making it work

LESSON

15

How are watts different from volts?

Words to know:

voltage

power

electrical power

A lthough batteries and power plants can produce extra electrons, current does not flow unless there is an electrical force to push the electrons. This electrical force is called voltage—a term named in honor of Alessandro Volta, the inventor of the first battery.

You can think of a battery like a water pump, but instead of pumping water, it pumps electrons. Just as water flows from a high place to a low place, so electrons flow from an area of higher electrical potential energy to an area of lower electrical potential energy. The negative electrode of a battery resists gaining more electrons, but easily gives off electrons so it has a high electrical potential. The positive electrode of a battery easily accepts electrons so it has a low electrical potential. Therefore, if a path is provided, electrons will easily flow from the negative to the positive side of a battery.

The greater the difference in electrical charge between the positive and negative electrodes, the greater the electrical force. This difference in potential energy is measured in units called volts. One volt can push 6.24×10^{18} electrons using 1 joule of energy. Two volts can push twice as many electrons, so the higher the voltage, the more current (electrons) that can be pushed in a given time period.

The flow of electrons alone is not very useful from a human perspective. The electrons must be used to perform some sort of work in order to be useful. Therefore, something other than a wire must be part of the circuit. This could be any electrical device. One of the simplest devices to understand is the electric light bulb. As current flows through the filament of the bulb, some of the current is transformed into light and heat energy. This is useful work. In other electronic devices, current is transformed into sound or mechanical movement. In a com-

BUILDING CIRCUITS

Purpose: To build a simple circuit

Materials: battery, copper wire, light bulb

Procedure:

1. Tape a copper wire to each end of a battery.

2. Next, tape the other end of one wire to the side of the metal connector on a light bulb, and tape the other end of the second wire to the bottom of the light bulb.

3. This setup allows current to flow from the negative terminal of the battery, through the light bulb, and back to the positive terminal of the battery.

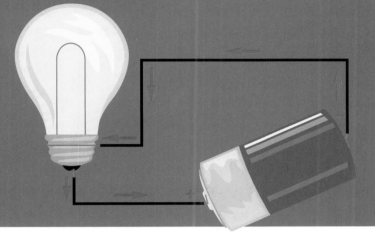

puter, current and voltage are used to store and transfer information.

Power is a measure of how fast work can be accomplished. It is measured in units called watts. A watt is 1 joule of energy per second. The power of a circuit is determined by the voltage (V) and the current (I). This relationship is shown as $P = IV$. **Electrical power** is equal to the voltage times the current. To help you understand this relationship, think about two light bulbs. A 60-watt bulb is brighter than a 40-watt bulb. Why? Because it uses more power. The voltage coming into your house is the same regardless of what it is attached to. The standard voltage in the United States is 120 volts. In order for a light bulb to use more power, it must allow more current per second to pass through. Therefore, the 60-watt bulb is using more current, so it can give off more light than the 40-watt bulb.

Going back to our analogy, you can think of current like water flowing downhill, voltage as the pump pushing the water up to the top of the hill, and power is the total volume of water that flows past a point in a given time period.

To protect circuit components from a sudden increase in current, many circuits contain fuses or breakers. A fuse is a component that contains a thin piece of wire. If too much current flows through the circuit, the wire will melt and open the circuit, thus protecting other components

The breaker box in your home protects your lights and appliances.

further down the line. The fuse must be replaced before current can again flow through the circuit. A breaker serves the same function, but a breaker is a switch instead of a thin piece of wire. If too much current flows through the breaker, the switch changes position, opening the circuit and stopping the current from flowing. The breaker must be reset before current can again flow. These devices prevent too much current from damaging other parts of the circuit. ■

WHAT DID WE LEARN?

- What is voltage?
- What direction does current flow in a battery?

TAKING IT FURTHER

- Explain how voltage is like a pump for electrons?
- Explain the difference between power and voltage.
- When might a fuse or a circuit breaker be needed?

BURGLAR ALARM

Complete the "Calculating Power" worksheet, then design a burglar alarm that will notify you if someone steps in front of a door or window. Think about what you have learned about current and switches. Draw a picture of your circuit. If you have the parts, you can build and test your circuit as well.

A home alarm system

SERIAL & PARALLEL CIRCUITS

Connecting the pieces

What's the difference between serial and parallel circuits?

Words to know:

resistance

serial circuit

parallel circuit

In the previous lesson we learned that a 60-watt light bulb is brighter than a 40-watt light bulb because more current passes through it in the same amount of time. But why does more current flow through the higher-powered bulb? To understand this you need to understand the idea of resistance.

Each material has a certain **resistance** to the flow of electrons. Copper metal has practically no resistance and is therefore a good conductor of electricity. Insulators such as paper, glass, and ceramic have high resistance to current. If you think about our analogy of current being like water, resistance is equivalent to the size of the pipe that the water is flowing through. A good conductor is a very wide pipe, so water (current) easily flows through it. An insulator is a very tiny pipe so only a very small amount of water (current) will flow through it. In our light bulb example, the 40-watt bulb is made with a material that has a higher resistance than the 60-watt bulb, therefore, less current will flow through it.

Placing something that resists current flow in the path of the current is how we get the current to do work for us. We have already seen how this works with light bulbs. But this works with other items as well. For example, the resistance of a heating coil in your oven converts the current into heat, thus enabling you to cook your food.

Electrical circuits can be set up in one of two ways depending on how the resistance is placed in the circuit. The simplest circuit is a circle and this is called a **serial circuit**. The current begins at the negative terminal of the battery. It flows through the first resistance, such as a light bulb. Then it flows through the second resistance, and so on until it finally flows back to the positive terminal of

BUILDING MORE COMPLEX CIRCUITS

Purpose: To build serial and parallel circuits

Materials: battery, wire, tape, three light bulbs

Procedure:

1. Build a serial circuit like the one pictured below. There should be only one path for the current to flow through. You may need to tape two batteries together to provide enough current to light all the light bulbs.

2. Once the lights are on, remove one light bulb from the circuit.

3. Now, reconnect the wire with only two light bulbs and observe any change in the bulbs.

4. Now use the same components to build a parallel circuit like the one pictured on the next page. There should be three paths for the current to flow through.

5. Again, remove one of the bulbs from the circuit.

Questions:

- What happened to the other light bulbs when you removed one in the serial circuit?

- What change did you notice in the brightness of the remaining light bulbs when you reconnected them? Why did they become brighter?

- What happened to the remaining bulbs when one was removed from the parallel circuit?

- Why did the remaining bulbs stay lit? Why didn't they become brighter?

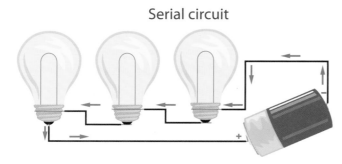

Serial circuit

the battery. There is only one path for the current to follow in a serial circuit.

The second type of circuit is called a **parallel circuit**. In this type of circuit, multiple paths exist for the current to follow. One side of each resistance is connected together at the negative terminal of the battery. The other side of each resistance is connected together at the positive terminal of the battery. See the diagrams here to better understand the difference between serial and parallel circuits.

Current, just like water, will take the path of least resistance. Therefore, in a parallel circuit, if there are two resistances that are the same, the same amount of current will flow through each. But if one item has a higher resistance than the other, more current will flow through the item with the lower resistance. ■

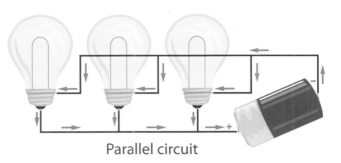

Parallel circuit

WHAT DID WE LEARN?

- Describe the difference between a serial circuit and a parallel circuit.

TAKING IT FURTHER

- How is electrical resistance similar to the diameter of a pipe for water?

- Which type of circuit would be best to use for a string of Christmas lights? Why?

OHM'S LAW

A physicist named Georg Simon Ohm determined that there is a direct relationship between the voltage potential, the current, and the resistance of a circuit. He determined that the relationship could be expressed as V=IR, where V is voltage, I is current, and R is resistance. The voltage is equal to the current times the resistance. In honor of his work, this relationship has been named Ohm's law and the units of resistance are called ohms.

Using this information, answer the questions on the "Voltage/Current" worksheet.

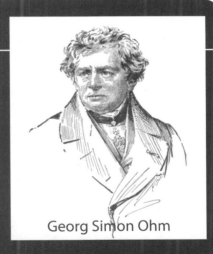

Georg Simon Ohm

UNIT 4

MAGNETISM

MAGNETIC FIELDS

What's a magnet?

LESSON
17

How do magnets work?

Words to know:

magnetism

magnetic moment

magnetic north pole

law of magnetic poles

Magnetism is a force that has baffled people for centuries. In ancient Greece, people knew that certain stones attracted bits of iron. They called these mysterious stones lodestone. But they did not really understand what caused this phenomenon, so for centuries magnetism was considered magic. In the Middle Ages, people started using the properties of magnets to form crude compasses for navigation. And in 1269 a man named Petrus Peregrinus de Maricourt discovered that magnets had poles. He noticed that iron filings were concentrated at opposite ends of a piece of lodestone. But people didn't really begin to understand magnetism until an Englishman named William Gilbert published a book of facts about magnets, listing all the then-known characteristics of magnets. Some of his "facts" were later proven wrong; nevertheless, his book did much to advance the use and understanding of magnetism.

Today we know that magnetism is not magic at all. Magnetism is an attractive or repulsive force that is contained in magnetic materials.

Everything around you is made up of tiny particles called *atoms*. Atoms contain other smaller particles, one of which is the electron. These electrons are very small—you can't even see them with the most powerful of microscopes. As the name might suggest, electrons have an electrical charge. And whenever electricity moves, a magnetic field is created.

Each electron generates its own tiny magnetic field, called a magnetic moment. The number of electrons and the way in which the north and south "poles" of their magnetic moments align determine the magnetic properties of the material. Most materials have an even number of paired electrons whose magnetic moments cancel each other out—they are not magnetic. However,

STUDYING MAGNETIC FIELDS

Purpose: To understand the magnetic field of a magnet

Materials: piece of paper, bar magnet, other magnets, iron filings, bowl, straight pins or paper clips

Activity 1—Procedure:

1. Place a plain sheet of paper over a magnet and carefully sprinkle iron filings onto the paper. The filings will be attracted to the magnetic poles and will reveal the lines of the magnetic field.

2. If you have more than one shape or type of magnet, look at each magnetic field separately.

3. On a separate piece of paper, sketch the shape of the magnet and the field that you observe for each magnet. The field generated by a bar magnet will look very different from the field generated by a horseshoe magnet.

4. After looking at the individual fields, connect two or more magnets together and view the field generated by this new magnet. Again, sketch the field that you observe.

Activity 2—Procedure:

1. Using a bar magnet with one end north and the other end south, tie a string to the magnet.

2. Slowly lower the magnet into a bowl of straight pins or paper clips. Slowly raise the magnet. How are the pins arranged on the magnet? Are they evenly distributed, or are they concentrated in one or more areas?

Activity 3—Procedure:

If you have more than one magnet, test the law of magnetic poles by trying to connect the magnets in different ways. You will find that the magnets attract when opposite poles line up, but if you turn one magnet around, the magnets will push each other apart. Even if you are strong enough to force the magnets together, they will pop apart as soon as you let go of them.

Activity 4—Procedure:

1. Hold a magnet above the table and connect a straight pin to the magnet.

2. Add a second pin to the end of the first pin. Why does it stick?

3. See how many pins you can add in a chain. Why can't you keep adding pins indefinitely?

Conclusion: Items made out of iron or steel, which is mostly iron, are attracted to magnets. When a steel object gets close enough to a magnetic field, its atoms become aligned with the magnetic field. This essentially turns the item into a magnet.

Magnetism

when the north and south "poles" of the unpaired electrons line up in the same direction and generate a magnetic field, a magnet is the result, the kind that sticks to your refrigerator.

One end of the magnet is called the north pole because that end of a magnet will align itself with the earth's magnetic north pole. And the other end of the magnet is called the south pole.

We learned in our study of electricity that opposite electrical charges attract and similar charges repel. The same is true for magnetic fields. Opposite poles attract and similar poles repel. So magnets line up north to south. This is called the law of magnetic poles.

Magnetic materials generate a field around them. The field is strongest near the poles and decreases with the distance from the poles. This field can be used in many ways. One way that magnetism is used is for pushing or pulling other magnetic items. Also, as we will learn in later lessons, magnetism is closely associated with electricity and these two forms of energy can be easily converted back and forth. ∎

WHAT DID WE LEARN?

- What is a magnet?
- Is the strength of a magnet the same throughout the magnet?
- What is the law of magnetic poles?

TAKING IT FURTHER

- Why does one pin stick to another when the first pin is attached to a magnet, even if they are not attracted to each other away from the magnet?

OBSERVING MAGNETIC FIELDS

Purpose: To demonstrate how current flowing through a wire will generate a magnetic field

Materials: wire, piece of paper, battery, iron filings, pencil, scissors

Procedure:

1. Poke a wire through the center of a piece of paper.

2. Bend each end of the wire and connect them to each end of a battery.

3. Sprinkle iron filings on the paper to see the magnetic field.

4. Now remove the wire from the paper.

5. Wrap it around a pencil or other round object several times to coil it, then remove it.

6. Cut a piece of paper so that it slips through the coil.

7. Connect the ends of the wire to a battery and sprinkle iron filings on the paper to see the magnetic field.

Question: What differences did you notice in the magnetic field between the coiled and straight wires?

Conclusion: The magnetic field is increased when the wire is coiled.

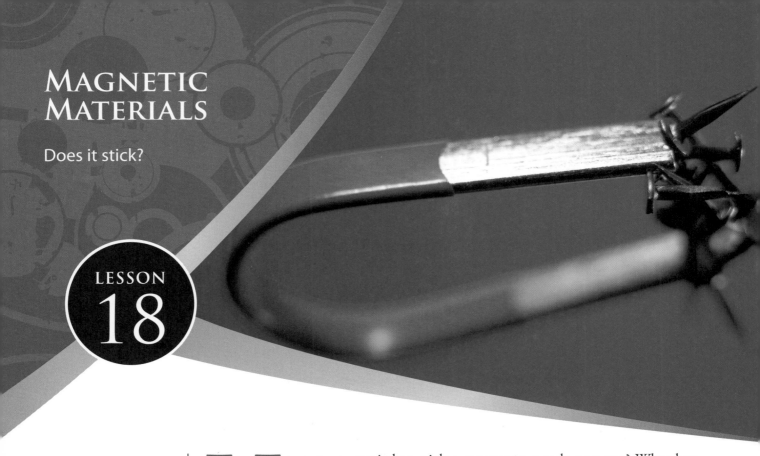

MAGNETIC MATERIALS

Does it stick?

LESSON 18

What kinds of materials are magnetic?

Words to know:

ferromagnet

paramagnetic

diamagnetic

nonmagnetic

Have you ever tried to stick a magnet to a soda pop can? What happened? It probably slid right off. However, we often use magnets to stick things to the front of our refrigerators. Why do magnets stick to some items and not to others? Recall that magnets are formed when most of the atoms line up in the same magnetic orientation. Only a few materials have atoms that easily line up in this way. Iron is the most common magnetic material. Other materials that are magnetic include cobalt, nickel, and gadolinium. Alloys that contain these materials can also be magnetic. For example: steel, which is a combination of iron and carbon, is magnetic because of its high iron content.

Materials that have a strong attraction to magnets are often called **ferromagnets**, from the Latin word *ferrous*, which means iron. Most items that are attracted to magnets contain iron. Some materials do not have an attraction to magnets, but they do have a slight effect on the magnetic field of the magnet. These materials are called **paramagnetic** materials. Paramagnetic materials include wood and aluminum. You can't get a magnet to stick to an aluminum can, but if you were able to measure the strength of the magnet's magnetic field, you would find that the can is very slightly attracted to the magnet. Finally, many materials are not at all attracted to magnets and are called **diamagnetic**, or **nonmagnetic**, materials. Salt and mercury are nonmagnetic.

Not all magnetic materials have the same magnetic strength. Some magnets are much stronger than others. Also, magnets can become weaker over time. To help maintain a magnet's strength, it is a good idea to store two magnets together with opposite poles matched. This helps the atoms in the magnets to maintain their orientation. Because a magnetic field is generated when the atoms all line up, if a

TESTING FOR MAGNETIC MATERIALS

Materials: iron nail, steel BBs, aluminum foil, plastic, paper, wood, penny, glass, two magnets, paper clip

Activity 1

Purpose: To test the magnetic properties of various materials

Procedure:

Test the following items to see if they are attracted to a magnet: iron nail, steel BBs, aluminum foil, plastic, paper, wood, a penny, and glass. Which of these items contain iron?

Activity 2

Purpose: To test the strength of two magnets

Procedure:

1. Slowly lower a magnet over a paper clip until the clip is attracted to the magnet.

2. Measure the height at which the paper clip began to move toward the magnet.

3. Repeat this with a different magnet. Which magnet could attract the paper clip at the furthest distance? This is the stronger magnet.

Activity 3

Purpose: To make a temporary magnet

Procedure:

1. Test an iron nail to see if it is magnetic by seeing if it will attract a paper clip.

2. If it is not, stroke the nail several times along your strongest magnet.

3. Now test to see if it is magnetic. You should be able to magnetize the nail if your magnet is strong enough.

magnet experiences a sharp blow, the magnet can lose its magnetism when the atoms become jumbled.

Some materials that are attracted to magnets can be induced to become magnets themselves. If an iron nail is stroked along a strong magnet, the atoms in the nail will be forced to align with the magnet's field and will thus cause the nail to become a magnet. This alignment will last for a short time or until the nail is struck and the atoms again become randomly aligned. A strong magnet can also change the orientation of a weaker magnet. So be careful not to place a magnet too close to your compass or it may lose its orientation. Also, never place magnets near TVs, computers, computer disks, or tapes that store magnetic information. ■

WHAT DID WE LEARN?

- What materials are magnetic?
- How can a magnet lose its magnetism?
- Do all magnetic materials produce the same strength of magnetic field?

TAKING IT FURTHER

- How can you make a magnet?
- Test a nickel coin to see if it is magnetic. Why doesn't a nickel stick to a magnet if nickel is a magnetic material?

STRENGTH OF MAGNETS

Design another way to test the relative strength of your magnets.

THE EARTH'S MAGNETIC FIELD

Is north really north?

Magnetism

What causes the earth's magnetic field?

Words to know:

Van Allen belts

Challenge words:

aurora borealis

aurora australis

aurora oval

solar maximum

solar minimum

The earth acts like a giant magnet. It has a magnetic field and north and south magnetic poles just like a magnet does. The earth's magnetic field, called the magnetosphere, extends thousands of miles out into space and plays a very important role in protecting the earth. Dr. James Van Allen built a radiation counter in 1958 and sent it into space on the Explorer I satellite. He discovered that the radiation count increased dramatically in the space around the earth. Further exploration revealed that the earth's magnetic field generates two donut shaped regions around the earth, one inside the other. These are called the Van Allen belts (shown at right). These fields trap harmful radiation in the form of charged particles from the sun and thus protect the earth. This is only one of the many ways that God designed the earth to protect the life He created here.

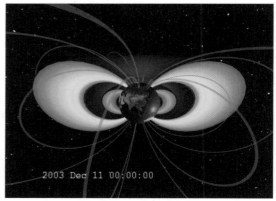

2003 Dec 11 00:00:00

How this magnetic field is generated is a subject of much debate. Most scientists believe that the core of the earth is made of solid iron, or mostly iron and nickel, surrounded by a liquid outer core and that the earth's magnetic field arises from convection currents in the liquid outer core, a good conductor of electricity. More recently, geophysicist J. Marvin Herndon proposed the idea that at the center of the earth there is a naturally occurring nuclear-fission reactor, five miles in diameter, which provides the energy needed to generate and sustain the earth's magnetic field. His theory is not commonly accepted; however, it is still being explored.

The earth's magnetic poles do not correspond to the geographic north and south poles about which the earth rotates. The earth's magnetic north pole is actually located north of Resolute Bay, Canada, in the Arctic Ocean. This point is about 1,200 miles (1,900 km) south of the geographic North Pole. So if you use a compass in Alaska, the needle will point northeast instead of north; and at the northernmost point of Greenland, a compass needle will actually point southwest. The magnetic north pole is not stationary. It is constantly moving northward at an average of between 6 and 25 miles per year (10–40 km/yr).

When we talk about the earth's magnetic north pole, we are talking about the area on the earth that the north pole of a magnet would point to or be attracted to. This can be a little confusing since the north pole of a magnet is attracted to the south pole of another magnet. So the earth's magnetic north pole would actually correspond to the south pole of a magnet.

The earth's magnetic field is decreasing a little each year. Observations and measurements of the earth's magnetic field have been made since 1835, and it is clear that the earth's magnetic field is decreasing. If this decrease has been constant in the past, this would indicate that the earth is much younger than most evolutionists believe it to be. At the current rate of decay, the magnetic field of the earth would lose half its energy about every 1,460 years. If the rate of decay is constant, the magnetic field would have been so strong only 20,000 years ago that it would have caused massive heating in the earth's crust and would have killed all life on earth. This supports the idea of an earth that is only about 6,000 years old, as indicated in the Bible.

Another source of much controversy is the switching of the polarity of the magnetic

MAKING YOUR OWN COMPASS

In addition to protection, one of the most common uses of the earth's magnetic field is for navigation with a compass. For hundreds of years, sailors have used a compass to help navigate, especially when stars were not visible. A compass works because a needle that is magnetized and allowed to float freely will point to magnetic north.

Purpose: To make your own compass

Materials: bowl, piece of paper, sewing needle, strong magnet, sponge, compass

Procedure:

1. Using a bowl, trace a circle on a piece of paper.

2. Use a ruler or straight edge to draw lines to divide the circle into four equal parts. Make the lines extend about 2 inches past the edge of the circle.

3. Label the top of one line with an N and the bottom of that line with an S. Label the left edge of the other line with a W and the right edge with an E.

4. Place the paper beneath the bowl and pour a small amount of water into the bowl.

5. Next, magnetize a sewing needle by stroking it against a strong magnet to cause the atoms to align with the magnet's magnetic field.

6. Place the needle on a small piece of sponge, about 1/2-inch square, and set it on the water. After several seconds, the needle should point to magnetic north.

7. Turn the piece of paper under the bowl so that the N lines up with the needle. Now you have a compass. Check the accuracy of your homemade compass with a real compass if you have one.

poles. Many magnetic rocks found inside the earth indicate that the north and south poles of the earth's magnetic field have switched several times in the past. Secular scientists date these polarity switches at an average of every 200,000 to 400,000 years, with the last reversal occurring about 700,000 years ago. However, creationists believe that these polarity switches most likely occurred during the Flood when the tectonic plates were moving rapidly. Creationists propose that the magnetic field stabilized after the Flood and has been steadily decreasing since that time. At the current rate of decay, the earth's magnetic field could collapse in about 3,000–10,000 years.

Regardless of the controversies surrounding the magnetic field of the earth, we know that God placed it there to protect the earth from harmful radiation and we can be thankful for it. ∎

WHAT DID WE LEARN?

- How is the earth like a giant magnet?
- How far does the earth's magnetic field extend?
- Where is the earth's magnetic north pole?

TAKING IT FURTHER

- What are some important uses of the earth's magnetic field?
- What technology has greatly replaced the need for compasses in navigation?

THE NORTHERN LIGHTS

As you just learned, the donut-shaped magnetic fields surrounding the earth are called the Van Allen belts. Radiation from the sun gets trapped in these belts. These charged particles move through the belts toward the poles. Near the poles, some particles escape into the lower atmosphere. When they collide with other particles in the atmosphere they give off a beautiful light often called the northern lights, or **aurora borealis**, near the North Pole, and the southern lights, or **aurora australis**, near the South Pole. There is an oval band called the **aurora oval** around each pole where the auroras can be seen that can extend from the poles to approximately 67 degrees latitude.

This band varies with the time of day and the time of year.

When the sun experiences solar flares a higher concentration of particles becomes trapped in the magnetosphere and the northern lights and southern lights are more visible. The sun experiences cyclic sunspot activity. Over a period of approximately 11 years, the sunspot activity cycles from very high to relatively low. When the sun is experiencing a very high level of sunspot activity it is called **solar maximum**. When the sunspot activity is lowest it is called **solar minimum**. The aurora activity can drop by as much as 30% between solar maximum and solar minimum.

On the average, the northern lights occur at an altitude between 325 and 400 feet (100–120 m). Some auroras have occurred at altitudes as high as 1,600 feet (500 m). The color of the lights is closely related to the altitude at which they originate. If the lights originate between 400 and 500 feet (120–150 m) the lights are usually green. Red lights originate at higher altitudes and blue and violet lights originate at altitudes below 400 feet (120 m).

If you have access to the Internet, you can do an image search for northern lights and see some amazing pictures of this beautiful phenomenon. As a bonus, see if you can find out who first gave this phenomenon its name.

ELECTRO-MAGNETISM

Creating a magnetic field

How is magnetism related to electricity?

Words to know:

electromagnet

As you have already learned, magnetism and electricity are very closely related forms of energy. Magnetic fields are formed when atoms line up in a particular way. This means that their electrons are lined up in a particular way to form the fields. Electricity is also related to electrons and occurs when electrons flow through a material. Therefore, it is reasonable to think that electricity and magnetism are related to each other.

This relationship was accidentally discovered by a Danish physicist named Hans Christian Oersted in 1819. Oersted found that a wire with a current flowing through it generated a magnetic field. A French scientist, Andre Marie Ampere, took this information and did further experiments. He discovered that a wire with a current flowing through it attracted a magnet if the current was flowing one direction and repelled the magnet if the current was flowing in the opposite direction.

It was later discovered that the magnetic field generated increased if the wire was coiled. The field increased even more if a magnetic material, such as iron, was placed in the middle of the coils. This arrangement is called an **electromagnet** and is used in many applications today.

Earlier we learned about the maglev trains that are using electromagnets to generate magnetic fields that move trains. Giant electromagnets are also

FUN FACT

The Japanese design for maglev trains uses liquid helium to super cool the magnets. This creates super magnets that are extremely efficient. Research is being done to try to create super magnets at room temperature. This would greatly reduce the costs of maglev trains and many other applications as well.

Magnetism

MAKING AN ELECTROMAGNET

Using the "Electromagnetism" worksheet, build and test your own electromagnet.

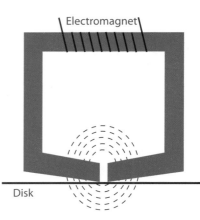

used in scrap yards to pick up and move large pieces of metal, including cars. Electromagnets are used to sort iron from other nonmagnetic metals such as aluminum. Also, electromagnets are used as electronic switches. You probably have an electromagnet in your doorbell.

Probably one of the most common uses of electromagnets is in videotapes, audiotapes, and computer disks. Videotapes, audiotapes, and computer hard drives all use electromagnets to store and play back information. The sound, picture, data, etc., are translated into electrical currents. The current is passed through an electromagnet, which generates a magnetic field. This field causes the magnetic material on the tape or hard drive to line up with the field. When the electromagnet is shut off, that data is stored in the magnetic material on the tape or disk. To retrieve the data, the tape or disk is passed under the electromagnet. The magnetic field on the tape induces a current to flow in the electromagnet and that current is then translated back into the original sound, picture, or other information that had been stored. ■

WHAT DID WE LEARN?

- What is an electromagnet?
- What are some common uses for electromagnets?

TAKING IT FURTHER

- How can you increase the strength of an electromagnet?
- What problems might occur if you increase the strength of an electromagnet?

POLARITY

Ampère discovered that the polarity of the magnetic field generated by an electromagnet is determined by the direction the current is flowing through the wire.

Purpose: To demonstrate how direction of current affects polarity of the magnetic field

Materials: electromagnet that you built, compass

Procedure:

1. Hold your electromagnet near a compass. Be sure not to touch the magnet to the compass. Note how the needle moves when the electromagnet is near.

2. Now, reverse the wires on the battery so that current is flowing the opposite direction. How did this affect the direction of the compass needle?

JOSEPH HENRY

1797–1878

Today most people don't know who Joseph Henry was or anything about him, but in his day he was considered the top American scientist, and his work was very important to the start of electronic communications. Joseph Henry was born to two Scottish immigrants that came to the United States in 1775, just before the start of the American Revolution. His father died when Henry was a small boy, and because the family had little money, Henry went to live with his grandmother in Galway, New York. At thirteen he was apprenticed to a watchmaker. Around that time, Henry became interested in theater. He was quite good and for a time became a professional actor.

In 1819 a friend talked Joseph into moving back to Albany and attending the Albany Academy where the tuition was free. To support himself, he traveled around the local area tutoring children. Even after he graduated from Albany Academy, he worked as a district schoolteacher and private tutor. At the Academy, Henry's interests turned to science, and by 1823 he started to assist in teaching science courses. Only three years later he was appointed professor of mathematics and natural philosophy. Even though he was very busy teaching seven hours a day, Henry still spent time in the lab. He was very interested in magnetism and electromagnetism, which was a new field of science. In this lab he built his first working electromagnet, which could lift 750 pounds (340 kg) of iron. Later he built a new, larger electromagnet, which could lift 2,300 pounds (1,040 kg) of iron. It was the largest electromagnet in the world.

In 1831 Joseph Henry showed his class a device similar to a telegraph. He demonstrated the device by running a mile of wire around the classroom, then connecting and disconnecting the wire from a battery at one end and making a bell ring at the other end. This work helped influence Samuel Morse with his invention of the first commercial telegraph. His work also led to his discovery of induction—the concept that led to the development of the electric motor.

Henry was considered a very good teacher as well as a good scientist, and in the early 1830s he was hired as a professor by Princeton. In 1846 he accepted the position as secretary (head) of the new and yet unformed Smithsonian Institute. He used this position to advance science in America. He later became one of the original members of the National Academy of Sciences as well as its second president. He was also a trustee of Princeton and president of the American Association for the Advancement of Science. Not only was Joseph Henry a brilliant scientist, but he was also a committed Christian. When Henry died in 1878, his funeral was attended by the president of the United States with his cabinet, the chief justice and associate justices of the Supreme Court, and by many members of both houses of Congress. He was so admired that a larger-than-life statue of him was erected in front of the Smithsonian Institution Building.

GENERATORS & MOTORS

Using magnets for work

LESSON

21

How can we use magnets to get work done?

Words to know:

generator

motor

Magnetism

The discovery that current flowing through a wire produced a magnetic field led scientists to wonder if a magnetic field could be used to make current flow through a wire. In 1830, the American scientist Joseph Henry discovered that a changing magnetic field did indeed produce a flow of current in a nearby wire. This discovery led to many developments that have greatly influenced the way we live.

Once scientists discovered that magnetic forces could cause electrons to move, they began experimenting to find ways to efficiently produce electricity. They found that the faster the magnetic field changes, the faster the electrons move. So they devised ways to create a changing magnetic field. In order to create a changing magnetic field, either a magnet must move through a coil of wire, or a coil of wire must move through a magnetic field. Either situation will produce a flow of current. This is the main idea behind all modern power plants.

Modern electric **generators** have giant coils of wire that spin inside magnetic fields as shown in the diagram. Steam or water is used to turn the turbines, or shafts, that are connected to these coils of wire. The water can be heated to produce the steam in a number of different ways. Some power plants burn coal or oil; others use nuclear reactions, solar energy, or geothermal energy to produce the heat needed to turn water into steam. Hydroelectric power plants use gravity pulling water downhill to push the turbines. But regardless of the method used to turn the turbines, all power

OBSERVING AN ELECTRIC MOTOR

A motor is essentially the opposite of a generator. Whereas a generator converts mechanical energy into electricity, a motor converts electricity into mechanical energy. Both generators and motors use electromagnets to convert the energy.

If you have permission from your parents, open up a small appliance, such as a mixer, and look at the electric motor inside. **Be sure it is unplugged first!** Try to identify the various parts. Look for the wire bringing in the current, a magnet,

coils of wire near the magnet, and gears that translate the mechanical energy into the required directions for the useful work done by the appliance. Do not take the motor apart, and be sure to carefully reassemble your mom's mixer!

plants must move coils through magnetic fields to generate the electricity on which our society depends.

Another modern electrical device that uses this same principle is the electric motor. An electric motor uses changing current flowing through a coil inside a magnetic field to produce mechanical energy. In an electric motor, a coil of wire is mounted inside a permanent magnetic field. When current flows through this coil, it changes the field and this pushes the coil. The movement of the coil can be used in many ways. For example, this energy is used to turn the beaters on an electric mixer, to turn a drill bit, or to turn the fan in a hair dryer. Many of the appliances in our homes have electric motors that use electromagnetism to produce mechanical energy. ■

FUN FACT

The Itaipu Hydroelectric Power Plant is located on the Parana River between the countries of Brazil and Paraguay. It is the largest hydroelectric power plant in the world. The power plant's 18 generating units add up to a total production capacity of 12,600 MW (megawatts). The total U.S. hydropower capacity is about 95,000 MW from more than 2,000 hydropower plants.

Magnetism

WHAT DID WE LEARN?

- What is an electric generator?
- How do most large electric generators work?
- What is an electric motor?
- How does an electric motor work?

TAKING IT FURTHER

- List some similarities and some differences between a coal power plant and a nuclear power plant.
- List at least two factors that determine how much electricity is generated by an electric generator.

MAGNET GAME

Design a game or toy that uses magnets. Be creative, and remember that magnets can be used to move things or to create electricity that can be used in a variety of ways. Consider using switches, lights, and anything you have learned about electricity and magnetism.

UNIT 5

WAVES & SOUND

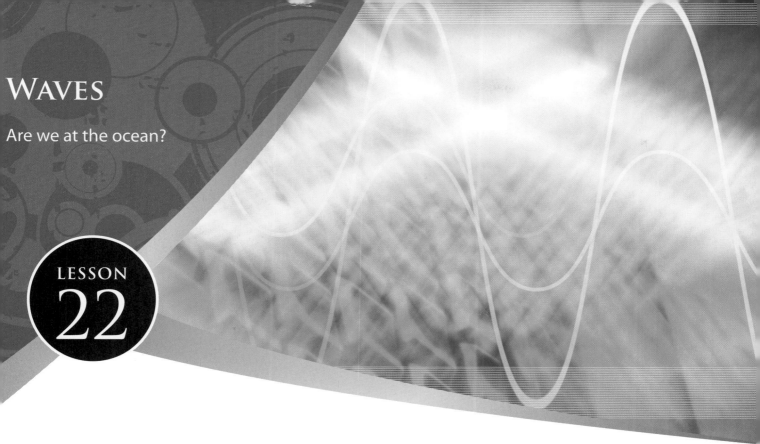

WAVES

Are we at the ocean?

What different kinds of waves are there?

Words to know:

waves

mechanical wave

electromagnetic wave

peak

crest

trough

wavelength

amplitude

cycle

frequency

velocity

Challenge words:

transverse wave

longitudinal wave

All of the forms of energy we have studied thus far—thermal, chemical, mechanical, nuclear, and electrical—transfer energy by changing the position of the particles or by changing the particles into a new substance. From boiling water to flying rockets, these forms of energy are all about moving and rearranging matter. Sound is another type of energy that involves the movement of particles through a medium (like air or water) but in a slightly different way.

Sound travels in **waves** as the particles bump into one another. This type of wave is called a **mechanical wave** because the particles must collide with one another, but the particles themselves move very little. This means that sound waves cannot travel through space because there are not enough particles in space to carry the sound. When you pluck a string on a guitar the vibration of the string causes the air molecules next to the string to vibrate. Each molecule of the air between your eardrum and the guitar string bumps into the next in a chain reaction in order for the sound energy to be transferred. Different strings on a guitar vibrate at different speeds and have more or less energy depending on how fast they vibrate.

Light also travels as a wave but does not require a medium, like air or water, to pass through. Light is one type of **electromagnetic wave**. Electromagnetic waves can transfer energy through empty space. The energy the earth receives from the sun is essential and can travel through the vacuum of space as X-rays, ultraviolet rays, visible light, and other forms. Visible light is the most recognizable form of electromagnetic energy, but radio waves, TV signals, microwaves, gamma rays, and infrared rays are all forms of electromagnetic waves.

There are several terms associated with energy that travels in waves. The

MAKING WAVES

Purpose: To observe waves

Materials: thin paper, rope, CD player or radio

Activity 1—Procedure:

1. Tape a 1-inch by 2-inch piece of paper around the center of a rope. Have one person hold one end of the rope stationary. Have another person give the other end of the rope one sharp shake up and down to make waves.

2. What happens to the piece of paper? This demonstrates how the energy of a sound wave can move through the molecules in the air without making the molecules move with it.

3. Increase how fast you move the rope up and down. What happens to the length of the waves? The waves are closer together. As the frequency increases, the wavelength becomes shorter.

4. Carefully watch the stationary end of the rope. What happens to the wave when it reaches the end? Can you see any of the energy reflected back along the rope in the other direction?

Activity 2—Procedure:

1. Tape a piece of tracing paper so that it hangs down over the speaker of a radio or CD player. Turn on some music. What happens to the paper?

2. Watch the differences in the vibrations as you increase and decrease the bass or treble in the music. How does the movement of the paper change as you increase or decrease the volume?

top of the wave is called the **peak** or the **crest**. The bottom of the wave is called the **trough**. The distance between two peaks is called the **wavelength**. And the height of the peak from the center of the wave is called the **amplitude**. All of these terms are important when describing sound, light, and other waves.

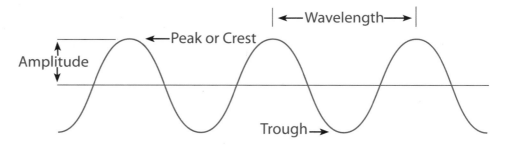

One wave is considered the energy from one peak to the next peak. This is sometimes called one **cycle**. If you count the number of peaks that pass a certain point in one second that number is called the **frequency** of the wave. Frequency is measured in units called hertz or cycles per second. Assuming the velocity of the wave remains the same, as the frequency goes up the wavelength must go down. This is called an inverse relationship—as one quantity goes up the other must go down. This means that if the wavelength is long, the frequency will be lower and if the wavelength of the wave is shorter, the frequency will be higher.

The **velocity**, or speed, of a wave is equal to its frequency times its wavelength. Sound waves travel at about 1,100 feet/second (300 meters per second) in air. Light travels much faster than sound at about 186,000 miles per second (300,000,000 m/s)—that's around a million times faster than sound! This is why you see lightning flash before you hear thunder, or see the beautiful lights of fireworks before you hear the boom.

Waves & Sound

Waves are energy and when waves encounter something that they cannot travel through, something must happen to that energy. What do you think happens to the energy? We know from the first law of thermodynamics that energy must be conserved, so the energy has to go somewhere. Sometimes the energy is absorbed and turned into heat energy. And sometimes it is reflected. Think about the water in a swimming pool. If you jump into the pool, you make waves in the water. When the waves reach the edge of the pool they reflect off the side of the pool and begin traveling back. Similarly, light and sound waves can be reflected off of different surfaces. Sound can be reflected off of the wall of a building or light can be reflected off of a mirror. We will discuss this more in later lessons. ■

FUN FACT

Light travels from the moon to the earth in about 1.3 seconds. Light travels from the sun to the earth in about 8.3 minutes.

WHAT DID WE LEARN?

- What is the main difference between mechanical and electromagnetic waves?
- What is the highest point of a wave called?
- What is the lowest part of the wave called?
- How is the wavelength of a wave defined?

TAKING IT FURTHER

- Which kinds of waves move faster, sound waves or light waves?
- What happens to a light wave when it hits a black surface?
- Can sound waves continue forever? If not, why not?

WAVE CHARACTERISTICS

Waves can be categorized by the way they travel with respect to the way they vibrate. **Transverse waves** travel at a 90° angle to the direction in which the vibration occurs. For example, the rope vibrates up and down but the wave moves from left to right. This is a transverse wave. Light waves move in this manner.

In other waves, the vibration occurs in the same direction in which the wave is moving. These waves are called **longitudinal waves**. In these waves, the vibrations move forward and backward as the energy of the wave moves forward. This can be demonstrated using a Slinky®.

Purpose: To observe transverse and longitudinal waves

Materials: metal spring toy (such as a Slinky®), "Wave Characteristics" worksheet

Procedure:

1. Have two people hold the ends of the Slinky® stationary.

2. Have a third person pull part of the Slinky® coils toward one end then let go. Watch as the energy moves back and forth along the Slinky®. This is how sound waves move. They compress and expand the air molecules ahead of them as they move forward through the air.

3. Complete the "Wave Characteristics" worksheet to better understand the terms wavelength, frequency, and velocity.

ELECTRO-MAGNETIC SPECTRUM

Different kinds of rays

LESSON 23

What are the various kinds of electromagnetic waves?

Words to know:

sound waves

ultrasound

radio waves

microwaves

infrared waves

visible spectrum

ultraviolet waves

X-rays

gamma rays

Challenge words:

analog signal

digital signal

Different energy waves travel at different frequencies. The frequency of the wave determines how different objects or materials respond to the waves. Sound waves are mechanical waves and must travel through some sort of medium such as air, wood, or water. These waves have frequencies between 20 and 20,000 hertz. These waves can be detected by the human ear and are thus designated as sound waves. Mechanical waves that have a frequency above 20,000 hertz are called ultrasound waves. They move in the same way as sound waves but cannot be heard by the human ear.

Electromagnetic waves have higher frequencies and do not require a medium through which to travel. In fact, they travel best through a vacuum. Most electromagnetic waves have frequencies from 100 kilohertz (100,000 Hz) to over 10^{25} hertz. Electromagnetic waves have both an electrical field and a magnetic field component, thus the name electromagnetic. We generally think of light waves when we think of these kinds of waves; however, the human eye can detect only a very narrow range of electromagnetic waves. Other electromagnetic waves include radio waves, X-rays, and gamma rays.

Radio waves, which include television signals, have frequencies between 100 kilohertz and 100 megahertz (100,000,000 Hz). Radio waves are used for various communications from military to ham radio, AM and FM radio, TV, and air traffic control signals. Antennas are used to generate the waves in this frequency range. The Federal Communication Commission (FCC) regulates generation of signals in the radio-wave range. The FCC determines which radio stations and TV stations can transmit in different areas of the United States. They also regulate the frequency and power at which the signals can be transmitted. This helps to prevent one signal from interfering with another signal.

Microwaves are energy waves in the frequency range from approximately 10^9 to 10^{11} hertz. Some communication signals are sent in the microwave range, but we are most familiar with using microwave technology to cook our food. Microwave ovens set up a changing electrical field. Water molecules are slightly positive on one side and slightly negative on the other side. Because of this, they flip back and forth trying to line up with the changing field. This movement causes other molecules to move and thus heats up your food.

In between the microwave range and the visible light range is the infrared energy range. **Infrared waves** quickly turn into heat when they hit most materials. Much of the energy from the sun is in the form of infrared waves. These waves hit the earth and help to warm it up. Although the human eye cannot see infrared waves, night vision goggles have been developed which can detect infrared waves and translate them into frequencies that can be detected by the eye.

Above the infrared range is the visible range of light. Visible light occurs in the frequency range from approximately 4.0×10^{14} Hz, which is red light, to 7.5×10^{14} Hz, which is violet light. Considering the full range of electromagnetic waves from 10^5 to 10^{25} hertz, the **visible spectrum** is a very small, but very important part. Visible light is given off by electrons in certain atoms. When energy is added to these atoms, some electrons are forced into a higher energy state than normal. When these electrons return to their natural state, they give off visible light. The frequency of the light determines its color. We will learn much more about visible light in later lessons.

Above the visible range of electromagnetic waves are the **ultraviolet rays**, **X-rays**, and **gamma rays**. All of these rays are very energetic and can damage body tissues if we are not careful. Ultraviolet rays from the sun can cause sunburn and even skin cancer. However, ultraviolet rays can also be used to kill harmful bacteria. X-rays can be used to see inside a human body to detect broken bones, cavities in teeth, and other ailments without having to invade the body. And gamma rays can be used to treat some forms of cancer by destroying the cancerous cells. God has designed a magnificent array of energy waves that man is just beginning to fully understand and use. The sun is the primary source of light on earth, and although it emits energy in all visible wavelengths of light, the sun also emits a large amount of energy at other wavelengths including infrared, ultraviolet, radio waves, and X-rays. ■

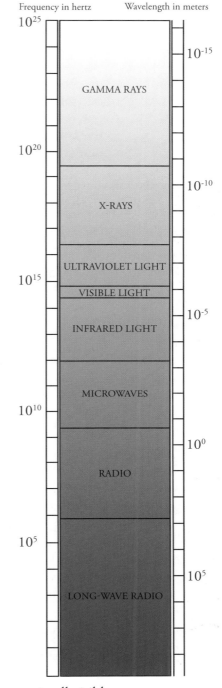

Frequency in hertz   Wavelength in meters

10^{25}

GAMMA RAYS

10^{20} 10^{-15}

X-RAYS 10^{-10}

ULTRAVIOLET LIGHT

10^{15} VISIBLE LIGHT

INFRARED LIGHT 10^{-5}

MICROWAVES

10^{10}

RADIO 10^{0}

10^{5}

LONG-WAVE RADIO 10^{5}

ELECTROMAGNETIC WAVES

Complete the "Electromagnetic Spectrum" worksheet.

Waves & Sound

FUN FACT

When we think of telescopes, we usually think of magnifying lenses that let us see distant planets and stars. However, many telescopes receive electromagnetic radiation outside of the visible spectrum. For example, radio telescopes are used to detect radio waves from space. These waves are then translated into pictures so we can "see" what is in the far reaches of the universe. Also, NASA is developing a new space telescope, called the James Webb Space Telescope (JWST), which will primarily detect infrared radiation from space.

WHAT DID WE LEARN?

- What characteristic of an electromagnetic wave determines its visible color?
- Which waves have a higher frequency, radio waves or gamma rays?
- Which kinds of electromagnetic waves are used for communication?

TAKING IT FURTHER

- Which electromagnetic waves can humans detect?
- Which color of light has the shortest wavelength?

Waves & Sound

RADIO AND TELEVISION

Radio and television signals are important forms of communication. These signals are transmitted as electromagnetic waves. The sound information is converted into an electrical signal and is imposed on top of a carrier signal. FM radio signals are ones that are frequency modulated. This means that the information is modulated, or changed, to match the frequency of the signal. AM radio signals are modulated, or changed, to match the amplitude of the signal.

TV signals are similar to radio signals except instead of only having sound information, a TV signal also carries picture information. About 350,000 pixels, or picture elements, are sent for each TV picture. The picture information is converted into electrical signals that control red, green, and blue "guns" in your TV picture screen, which cause different parts of the screen to light up.

Traditional TV and radio signals are **analog signals**. This means that the information is sent in the form of waves. However, newer technology now converts the sound and picture information into a series of 1s and 0s and transmits this digital information on the carrier signal instead. **Digital signals** can be compressed and sent at a faster rate than analog signals and are more accurate, thus producing a better TV image.

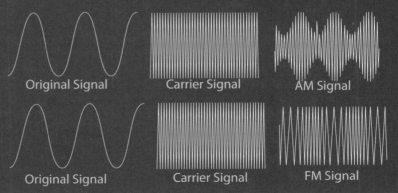

Original Signal   Carrier Signal   AM Signal

Original Signal   Carrier Signal   FM Signal

SOUND WAVES

Do you hear what I hear?

LESSON 24

How does sound travel?

Waves of energy that can be detected by the human ear are called sound waves. Sound waves are vibrations that are changed into electrical signals inside the ear. Sound waves cannot travel through empty space or a vacuum. Robert Boyle demonstrated this in 1660 by placing a watch with an alarm inside a glass case. When the air was pumped out, the alarm could not be heard, but as air was allowed back in, the alarm became audible and gradually grew louder.

Sound waves can travel through many substances. Humans generally hear sounds that travel through air. But swimmers hear sounds that travel through water. You can also detect sounds as they travel through metal, wood, and other materials. Some materials do not transmit sounds as well as others. Sound dampening materials are often used to insulate one area from another or to absorb sound waves. Cloth and other porous materials absorb sound waves. Porous materials are ones with air pockets. So to keep an office or other public area quiet, building designers often use carpet, padded walls, and other fabric-covered objects to absorb much of the sound that is generated.

Sound waves travel at different speeds through different materials. In air, sound waves travel at about 1,130 feet per second (330 m/sec). In water, sound waves travel faster, at about 4,790 feet/second (1,450 m/sec). Sound waves travel even more quickly through wood and iron than they do through air or water. The speed that the sound waves travel is also affected by the temperature of

FUN FACT

Young children can hear sounds in the frequency range from 20–20,000 hertz. As we age, we lose the ability to hear some frequencies, especially the higher frequencies.

HEARING THE SOUNDS

Purpose: To test which objects reflect sound and which absorb it

Materials: kitchen timer, two cardboard tubes, balloon

Activity 1—Procedure:

1. Have someone hold a beeping kitchen timer at one end of a cardboard tube so that the sound travels down the tube.

2. Have him/her point the other end of the tube at the wall.

3. Hold a second tube so that one end is pointing at the same spot on the wall and place your ear at the other end of the second tube.

4. Plug the ear that is not near the tube. Can you hear the beeping?

5. Unplug your ear. Does the sound seem louder through the tube than it is to your other ear?

6. Now point the tube with the timer at a couch or other cloth-covered object. Again, listen to the sound through the second tube. How is the beeping different from the sound you heard at the wall?

7. Try directing the sound toward different surfaces. Which surfaces reflect the sound? Which surfaces absorb the sound?

Activity 2—Procedure:

1. Hold the timer in the air and listen to the beeping.

2. Blow up a balloon and place the timer on one side of the balloon and listen to the beeping by placing your ear against the other side of the balloon. How does the beeping compare to the sound you heard through the air?

the medium through which they are moving. The warmer the medium, the more quickly its atoms are moving, and therefore the more quickly the sound waves can move through it. Density of the medium also affects the speed of the sound waves. Sound waves can travel more quickly through dense materials than through less dense materials. You may have seen an actor in a movie listening to a railroad rail to see if the train was coming or listening to the ground to see if an animal was approaching. This may seem silly, but sound travels faster through an iron rail or through the dense ground than through the air, so this idea is not so silly after all.

When we talk about sound waves, we often say that the waves travel through the medium without moving the particles or atoms of the medium. What this means is that the atoms do not travel with the wave. Remember when you moved the rope up and down? The paper did not travel down the rope. This shows that the atoms remain in about the same position after the wave goes through as they were in before the wave went through. However, it does not mean that the atoms did not move at all as the wave passed through. Just as the paper on the rope moved up and down, so also the atoms in the air or water move a slight amount as the sound wave passes through.

Sound waves travel through a medium by compressing then expanding the molecules of the medium. The compression corresponds to the peak of the wave and the expansion of the molecules corresponds to the trough of the wave. Thus, the air, water, or other molecules are vibrating back and forth as the sound wave passes through. On average, the vibration or movement of air molecules is less than 0.004 inches (1/10 of a millimeter).

FUN FACT

The longest known echo inside a building was measured in the Chapel of the Mausdeum in Hamilton, Scotland. When the door is closed in the building, its echo can be heard for 15 seconds.

Waves & Sound

Sound waves begin at a particular point in space. For example, you may drop a spoon on the floor and the impact causes vibrations at the point of impact. These vibrations move outward from the source in what would be similar to ripples in a pond. The sound moves out in all directions from the source until it hits something. The object it hits will either absorb the energy from the sound wave, or reflect that energy. The sound wave will continue moving until all of its energy has been absorbed and turned into another form of energy, such as heat.

Sound is a wonderful blessing. Consider how different life would be without all of the wonderful, and sometimes not so wonderful, sounds in the world. And you can praise God for designing your ear to be able to hear them all. ■

WHAT DID WE LEARN?

- What is a sound wave?
- How do sound waves move through the air?
- What are some materials through which sound waves can travel?
- What types of materials absorb sound waves?

TAKING IT FURTHER

- Can sound be heard in outer space?
- What could you do to help make a room quieter?
- If you blew a horn at the edge of a lake, who would hear the sound first, someone swimming underwater or someone the same distance away on the shore of the lake?
- Echoes occur when sound bounces off of different surfaces. What makes an echo stop?

SPEED OF SOUND

Purpose: To measure the speed of sound

Materials: stopwatch or watch, tape measure, "Speed of Sound" worksheet

Procedure:

1. Go outside to a location with a large smooth wall.

2. Shout toward the wall. Listen for an echo of your voice.

3. Step far enough away from the wall that the echo will take a noticeable time to be heard, at least 50 yards (45 m).

4. Shout and accurately measure how long it takes for the echo to reach your ears. Record your measurements on a copy of the "Speed of Sound" worksheet.

5. Use a tape measure to measure the distance from where you were standing to the wall. Record your measurements on your worksheet.

6. The distance that the sound traveled was twice the distance from you to the wall, since it had to get there and back. Now calculate the speed of sound using the following formula: Speed = Distance/Time. Complete your worksheet.

Conclusion: The speed of sound is usually about 1,130 ft/sec (330 m/s) in air, but this varies with the temperature of the air and with altitude, so your answer is probably different.

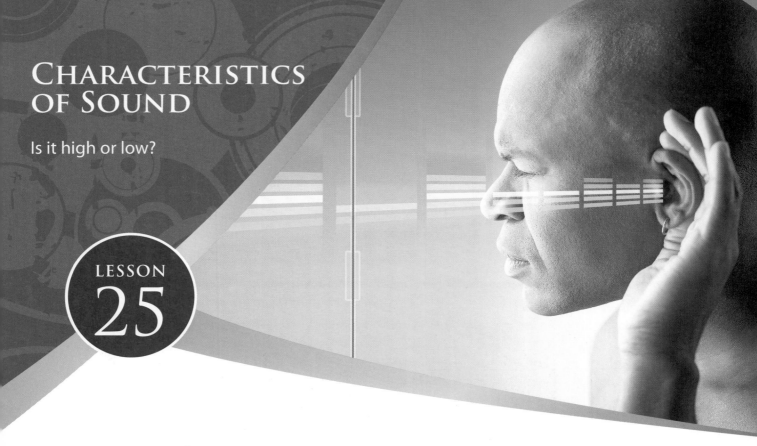

CHARACTERISTICS OF SOUND

Is it high or low?

LESSON 25

How can we make different sounds?

Words to know:

pitch

loudness

overtones

harmonics

We know that all sounds are not alike. One key on a piano may produce a very deep sound and another may make a high sound. This is because the various strings vibrate at different frequencies. The low sounds are made by thicker strings that vibrate more slowly than the thinner strings that make the higher sounds. The characteristic of high or low sound is called **pitch**. Pitch is directly related to the frequency of the sound wave vibration.

Another characteristic of sound is its loudness. **Loudness** is directly related to how high the peaks or crests of the wave are. This is called the amplitude of the wave. Amplitude is a result of the amount of energy that is in the wave. The more energy that is in the wave, the higher the amplitude of the wave and thus the louder the sound.

Alexander Graham Bell, inventor of the telephone, defined the unit of measurement for the loudness of sound as 1 bel. This unit does not allow for much distinction between volumes, so most sounds are described in terms of 1/10 of a bel, or a decibel. One decibel is the smallest difference in volume that the human ear can detect. A whisper is about 20 decibels, normal talking is about 60 decibels, and a jet engine is about 150 decibels. The threshold of pain is about 120 decibels, so standing next to a jet engine would definitely hurt your ears and probably do permanent damage to your hearing. In fact, permanent damage can occur when you hear sounds that are louder than 100 decibels.

Alexander Graham Bell

EXPERIMENTING WITH PITCH

Purpose: To make a simple instrument

Materials: rubber band, ruler, pencil

Procedure:

1. Stretch a rubber band over a ruler lengthwise.

2. Place a pencil under the rubber band near one end and place a finger on top of the rubber band where it passes over the pencil.

3. Now pluck the rubber band and listen to the pitch of the vibration.

4. Move the pencil closer to the middle of the ruler and again pluck the rubber band. How does the pitch change? What caused the pitch to change?

5. Move the pencil about 2/3 of the way down the ruler. Holding the rubber band in place against the pencil, pluck the short part of the rubber band. How does the pitch compare to the original pitch?

6. Try plucking the rubber band very lightly. Then pluck it again more strongly. Did the pitch change? When did you hear the loudest sound?

The third characteristic that determines the quality of sound is the overtones of the vibration. Overtones, also called harmonics, are waves that vibrate at some multiple of the fundamental frequency. When a string is hit on a piano, it begins to vibrate at a particular frequency. But that string also generates waves that are 2 times, 3 times, or other multiples of the main frequency. For example, if a note vibrates at a frequency of 440 Hz, its overtones could vibrate at 880 Hz or 1320 Hz. A sound wave may have only even multiples, only odd multiples, or any combination of multiples. The number and intensity of these overtones is what makes one instrument sound very different from another, even when they are playing the same note.

Sound is not a simple matter. The pitch, loudness, and overtones all play a part in the quality of the sound we hear. ■

Tuning forks are used to tune musical instruments. When struck against a surface, they resonate at a specific constant pitch, and emit a pure musical tone. The pitch that a particular tuning fork generates depends on the length of the two prongs.

Waves & Sound

WHAT DID WE LEARN?

- What are the three main characteristics that determine the quality of a sound?

- How does the pitch change as the frequency goes up?

- What is an overtone?

- What units are used to measure loudness?

TAKING IT FURTHER

- Is a shorter string likely to produce a higher or lower pitch than a longer string?

- Explain why a trumpet playing a C and a piano playing a C sound different.

- Why should you keep the volume of your music below 100 decibels?

AMPLIFYING SOUND

Sometimes you are not able to add more energy to a sound wave, yet you need to make it louder so you can hear it better. One way to do this is to gather more sound waves and concentrate them into one area. This is the idea behind a stethoscope.

Purpose: To make your own stethoscope

Materials: rubber or plastic tube, funnel

Procedure:

1. Attach a rubber or plastic tube to the small end of a funnel.

2. Hold the funnel up to something you want to listen to and put the other end of the tube close to your ear.

Conclusion: The sound should be louder through the tube than without it because the funnel collects sound waves and concentrates them. This gives them more energy and makes them louder.

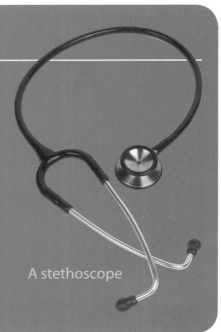

A stethoscope

STUDYING WAVES

As you have already learned, there are many different kinds of waves. However, in general, most waves behave in some similar ways.

When a wave encounters a surface that does not absorb it, the wave bounces off. This is called reflection. Because we cannot see light or sound waves, it is useful to study water waves to help us understand how these other waves behave.

Purpose: To observe how waves behave

Materials: bathtub, two bottles

Procedure:

1. Put 2–3 inches of water in a bathtub. Be sure that light is shining on the water; this will enable you to see the waves better.

2. Hold a bottle on its side and push it into the water near one edge of the tub. Observe how the waves travel across the tub and what happens to them when they reach the other side. Experiment with how hard and how far you push the bottle to achieve waves that are easy to see.

3. Now place a bottle upright in the far side of the tub, and generate more waves. Observe the waves that reflect off of the bottle.

4. Next, push some waves toward the corner of the tub.

Questions:

- What happened to the waves as they reached the straight sides of the tub?

- How do the waves reflect off of the curved surfaces of the bottle and the tub corners?

- How are the reflections different in the concave curve of the tub compared to the convex curve of the bottle?

BEHAVIOR OF SOUND

Fun with sound

What causes different sound effects?

Words to know:

acoustics

reverberation

resonance

Doppler effect

SONAR

Challenge words:

interference

constructive interference

destructive interference

Have you ever walked into a building where every sound echoed off the walls? Is your library a very quiet place? **Acoustics** describes a building's effect on the sounds within it. Sound waves reflect off of hard surfaces, whereas porous surfaces absorb some of the energy of the sound wave and thus help to reduce the sound. The use of a building will determine its acoustical design. For example, an office building will usually have carpet, cloth-covered walls or dividers, and soft furniture to absorb much of the sound generated by the people and machinery in the office. A library will also have these kinds of sound-absorbing materials to keep things quiet. However, the stage of a concert hall would not be designed this way. The hard surfaces of a concert hall are designed in such a way that they reflect the sound waves coming from the stage toward the audience so that the audience can enjoy the music.

Buildings that are not designed to absorb sound energy can experience reverberations. **Reverberations** are multiple echoes. Have you ever been in a noisy restaurant? Sometimes it seems that you can hear the conversation across the room better than you can hear the person sitting across the table from you. These reverberations must be controlled in a concert hall by using padded seats and cloth curtains so that the listener only hears the music once, and does not hear echoes of the music.

Sound has many interesting effects other than just reverberations and echoes. Another interesting sound effect is resonance. You learned in the last lesson that a string has a fundamental frequency. Its length, thickness, tension, and the material it is made from, determines this frequency. If two identical strings are close to each other and one string is made to vibrate, the energy from the vibrating string can cause the second string also to vibrate. This phenomenon is called

Waves & Sound

TESTING SOUND EFFECTS

Purpose: To create your own Doppler and other sound effects

Materials: cardboard tube, hole punch, string, stringed instrument, water goblet

Activity 1—Procedure:

1. Punch two holes opposite each other near the end of a cardboard or paper tube.

2. Tie a string that is 2–3 feet long through the holes of the tube.

3. Holding the end of the string, swing the tube around your head at a constant speed. Listen to the sound of the air passing through the tube. Does it stay the same as it goes around your head?

Activity 2—Procedure:

1. If you have a guitar or other stringed instrument, tune two adjacent strings to the same note.

2. Pluck one string and observe the second string. Some of the energy from the first string may make the second string begin to vibrate.

Activity 3—Procedure:

1. Obtain a water goblet, and clean your fingers.

2. Gently slide your finger over the rim of the water goblet. You might be able to set the goblet into vibration by means of stick-slip friction. (You may have to slightly wet your finger and keep trying for awhile.)

Conclusion:

Why does a crystal goblet "sing"? Like a bow being pulled across a violin string, the finger sticks to the glass molecules, pulling them apart at a given point until the tension becomes too great. The finger then slips off the glass and subsequently finds another microscopic surface to stick to; the finger pulls the molecules at that surface, slips and then sticks at another location. This process of slip-stick friction is sufficient to set the molecules into vibration at the glass's natural frequency.

resonance. Resonance occurs in many materials, not just between two strings. The energy of any vibrating material can be transferred to another material with the same natural frequency.

Resonance is very important in speaking, listening, and music. The sounds in your sinus cavities resonate and amplify your voice. Resonance in the auditory canal of your ear amplifies the sound to your eardrum. And the sound box on many instruments, primarily stringed instruments, amplifies the sound through resonance.

Another interesting sound effect is called the Doppler effect. In 1842 an Austrian physicist named Christian Doppler first noticed that light from distant objects in space was color shifted—the light was a different color than was expected. After much work, he was able to mathematically describe how this shift occurs. Later, he realized that this same effect occurs with sound. You may have noticed that the pitch of a siren changes as an ambulance approaches and then goes away from you. This is because of the Doppler effect.

If you are stationary and the sound source is moving toward you, the sound waves are pushed closer together in front of the moving object so the pitch increases as the object moves toward you. As the object moves away from you, the sound waves are stretched out behind the moving object, so its pitch becomes lower.

FUN FACT

Bats use the Doppler effect to determine the speed and direction of flying insects they wish to eat. Whales and dolphins can also use the Doppler effect to locate food.

A couple of other special sound effects are ones that are not used for the human ear. SONAR, SOund NAvigation and Ranging, is a system that measures how sound waves reflect off of distant objects. Sonar is most often used by ships to explore the bottom of the ocean. The ship sends out a sound wave, and then translates the reflected sound wave into a picture, giving a visible look at the objects under the sea. In a similar way, ultrasound waves, sound waves that are at a frequency too high for the ear to hear, are used to see a tiny baby still in its mother's womb. These sound waves bounce off the tiny body and are picked up by the machine. The machine translates them into a picture that shows the miracle of life inside the womb. ■

WHAT DID WE LEARN?

- What are acoustics?
- What is resonance?
- What is the Doppler effect as it relates to sound?

TAKING IT FURTHER

- How are sonar and ultrasound technologies similar?
- Give an example, other than a siren, when you have heard the Doppler effect?
- Does the driver of an ambulance hear the siren change pitch as he/she drives?
- Name some places you have been where it was easy to hear reverberations.

INTERFERENCE

Waves are traveling in the air all around us. Some we can see and hear, while others are invisible and undetectable by our bodies. Sometimes two traveling waves will meet and can affect each other. When one wave affects another it is called **interference**. If two waves at the same frequency are traveling in opposite directions they can meet. If two peaks meet at the same time, they will add and the amplitude of the wave will temporarily become twice as high. This type of interference is called **constructive interference**. If this happens with sound waves, the sound will temporarily become louder.

If two waves meet such that a peak and trough come together at the same time, they will cancel each other out. This is called **destructive interference**. Destructive interference will cause the sound to disappear where the interference is taking place.

Although we can't see most of the waves around us, we can observe waves in water that act the same way as sound, light, and radio waves.

Purpose: To observe interference in waves

Materials: bathtub

Procedure:

1. Fill a bathtub with 2–3 inches of water. Be sure that the surface of the water is well lit.

2. Once the surface is smooth, turn the faucet on so that water is slowly dripping into the tub.

3. Watch how the waves generated by the dripping water reflect off of the sides of the tub and how they affect each other.

Look for lighter and darker areas indicating constructive and destructive interference. Slightly increase the rate at which the water is dripping. What differences do you notice in the waves?

MUSICAL INSTRUMENTS

What do you play?

How do different instruments produce sound?

Words to know:

string instrument

percussion instrument

wind instrument

electronic instrument

Waves & Sound

Music is something that nearly everyone enjoys in one form or another. But what exactly is music? Music is regular vibrations of sound with definite pitches, as opposed to random vibrations of sound. Music is determined by seven distinct pitches in the musical scale. Each pitch has a designated frequency. For example, the note A vibrates at 440 hertz.

There are many ways to make music. One of the easiest ways to make music is to sing or hum. Singing occurs in your larynx. Air flowing across the vocal cords produces vibrations, which exit your mouth. The tighter you make your vocal cords the higher the pitch of the note. If you loosen the tension in your vocal cords, you will produce a lower-pitched note. You can place your hand on your throat and feel the vibrations in your voice box as you sing.

But, of course, not all music is produced by singing. Much of the music we hear is produced by musical instruments. There are four basic kinds of musical instruments: string, percussion, wind, and electronic instruments. **String instruments** produce sound when a stretched string is plucked, hit, or rubbed by a bow. In most stringed instruments, as the string vibrates the energy is transmitted to the bridge of the instrument. The bridge is the raised piece over which the strings are stretched. The bridge transmits the vibration to the front plate of the instrument, which in turn resonates inside the sound box, thus amplifying the sound.

The pitch of the string is determined by three factors: the length of the string, the tension of the string, and the mass of the string. A thick string will have a lower pitch than a thin string of the same length. A longer string will have a lower pitch than a shorter string of the same thickness. Musicians learn to change the tension and length of their instrument's strings in order to produce the many sounds needed for the music they want to create. You are probably familiar with many stringed instruments. Some common string instruments include violin, cello, double bass, guitar, harp, and banjo.

Percussion instruments are ones which produce a note when the surface of the instrument is struck by an object. The object could be a drumstick, a hammer, a mallet, or your hand. The physical size of the instrument is the main determining factor in the pitch and tone that it produces. You probably think of a drum when you think of a percussion instrument. But percussion instruments also include cymbals, bells, chimes, tambourine, xylophone, castanets, triangle, and maracas. The piano is usually considered a string instrument, although it is sometimes classified as a percussion instrument as well, because the strings are hit with hammers.

The third type of musical instrument is the wind instrument. **Wind instruments** are ones which produce a note when air is moved across a hole or reed. These vibrations are carried from the mouthpiece to a column of air inside the instrument. The tension of the musician's mouth and the length and volume of the column of air determine the pitch that is produced. The length of the column of air is changed by pressing valves or covering holes in the instrument.

Wind instruments are usually divided into two categories: brass and wood. Brass instruments, as you would expect, are made from brass. They generally produce very strong overtones and have a loud sound. Some common brass instruments include the trumpet, trombone, tuba, and French horn. Woodwinds are instruments that are often made from wood, but can be made from other materials as well. They tend to have a more mellow sound than brass instruments. Woodwind instruments you have probably seen include the clarinet, oboe, flute, saxophone, and piccolo. Others are less common including the bassoon, bagpipes, and the English horn.

Electronic instruments have been invented just in the past several decades. **Electronic instruments** produce electronic signals that can be converted into sound waves. Most of these instruments resemble the traditional instrument that they are trying to copy. For example, an electric guitar has strings like an acoustic guitar; however, it does not primarily amplify the vibrations of the strings. Instead, it converts

The flute is a woodwind instrument.

Waves & Sound

MAKING MUSIC

Purpose: To make and play your own instrument

Materials: glass jars or cups, spoon, soda straws, cardboard, empty tissue box, rubber bands

Water Xylophone

Procedure:

1. Fill several jars or glass cups with different amounts of water. Pour 2 tablespoons of water in the first glass or jar, ¼ cup of water in the next, ¼ cup plus 2 tablespoons in the third and so on.

2. Now tap the side of each jar or cup with a spoon. Each jar should produce a different pitch.

3. Try to play a tune using your new xylophone. Use two spoons to play multiple notes at one time. Adjust the level of the water if you want a higher or lower pitch.

Panpipes

A traditional wind instrument in Peru is called the panpipes. This is a series of wooden pipes of various lengths glued together side by side. By blowing across the pipes, the musician can make wonderful tunes.

Procedure:

1. Cut soda straws to various lengths.

2. Lay the straws side by side from shortest to longest, and glue them onto a 1 inch by 3 inch piece of cardboard with the tops of the "pipes" even with each other.

3. When the glue is dry, try blowing across the top of each straw. Each one will produce a different note.

Box Guitar

Procedure:

1. Cut a 2-inch diameter hole in the side of a small box or use an empty tissue box.

2. Stretch three or more rubber bands of different thicknesses around the box so that they go across the hole.

3. Now pluck the rubber bands. Each one should make a different sound.

4. Press one of the rubber bands against the box to shorten its length. Pluck the rubber band. How does its pitch compare to the full-length rubber band? (It should be higher.)

5. Try to play a song by adjusting the lengths of the rubber bands to achieve something close to the desired pitch for each note.

Bas-relief sculpture of an Egyptian playing the harp

the vibrations into an electrical signal that is then changed into sound waves through an amplifier and speaker. With the use of computers, electronic instruments can simulate nearly any musical sound. However, electronic music does not have the same richness as the more traditional musical instruments.

Musical instruments have been around since the beginning of man. In Genesis 4:19 it says that Jubal was the father of all who play the harp and flute. So we know that within just a short time after creation, musical instruments were being played. The harp is one of the oldest instruments. Not only is it mentioned in Genesis 4, but harps have been found in nearly every culture, and the oldest archeological records show harps in ancient Sumer, ancient Egypt, and ancient Babylon all more than 2,000 years ago. Another ancient instrument is the trumpet. Ancient trumpets were straight with no valves and were used at least 2,000 years ago in Egypt. The looped design for a trumpet was adopted in the 15th century and valves were added in the 1820s.

Other instruments are of more recent origin. The violin was invented in 1510. It descended from two other medieval instruments—one called the fiddle and the other the rebec. The first piano was made by Bartolomeo Cristofori in Florence, Italy, in 1698. Prior to that time most of what we would call piano music was played on a harpsichord. The harpsichord was similar to a piano, but the strings were plucked instead of being struck with hammers. The clarinet was invented by a man named Jacob Denner in 1710. The saxophone was created by Adolphe Sax in 1840. And John Phillip Sousa invented the sousaphone in 1898.

Music has many uses and infinite tunes. But the greatest use for music is to worship God. Psalm 150 says, "Praise Him with the sound of the trumpet; praise Him with the lute and harp! Praise Him with the timbrel and dance; praise Him with stringed instruments and flutes! Praise Him with loud cymbals; praise Him with clashing cymbals!"

So use your music, whether with an instrument or just your voice, to praise your awesome Creator. ■

FUN FACT

Three of the original pianos made by Bartolomeo Cristofori still exist. One made in 1720 is on display in New York. A 1722 piano is in Rome, and a 1726 piano is in Leipzig, Germany.

WHAT DID WE LEARN?

- What makes music different from noise?
- What are the four main types of instruments? How does each make a tone?
- What is one of the oldest musical instruments?

TAKING IT FURTHER

- How is your voice box, or larynx, like a musical instrument?
- Why is a piano sometimes considered to be a percussion instrument?
- How can a bugle make different notes if it does not have valves?
- How are string instruments tuned?
- How are wind instruments tuned?

DESIGN AN INSTRUMENT

Design and build your own musical instrument. For more fun, research the history of your favorite instrument.

Special FEATURE

JOHANN SEBASTIAN BACH

1685–1750

"All my music I wrote for God."—*J. S. Bach*

Johann Sebastian Bach was one of the most prolific composers of all time, yet his music was nearly lost to us. He is well known today for his beautiful piano music, yet he lived before the piano was a common instrument. Let's investigate how this famous composer became who he was.

Born the youngest son to Ambrosius Bach, who was a professional musician, Johann Sebastian was the most musically gifted of all his siblings—who were all musicians in their own right. Johann attended the same school that Martin Luther had studied at 200 years earlier. In order to graduate, a student had to memorize the Compendium, a 203-page document outlining Lutheran belief and practice, which Johann did. He was also reading the Bible in Latin by the age of 10.

During the 17th and 18th centuries, life was very hard, and the population in the Holy Roman Empire dropped from sixteen million to less than six million. Johann's family suffered along with the rest. Johann's mother died in 1693, when he was only 8, and then ten months later his father also died. The next year, Johann Sebastian and his bother Jacob were sent to live with their older bother Johann Christoph who was the organist at the church of St. Michael in Ohrdruf.

When Johann Sebastian was about 15, he and a friend went north on a 200-mile trek to a school of sorts where their duties were to sing in church in return for tuition, room and board, plus a small allowance. Johann had an incredible soprano voice and sang beautifully. Eventually his voice changed, but he was allowed to stay at the school because of his abilities on the organ.

Johann Sebastian's first employment was in a small town where he wrote "Gott ist Mein König" (God is My King). It was during this time he married his cousin Maria Barbara Bach, with whom he had seven children.

During Bach's lifetime, the area we call Germany was made up of about 300 small principalities, each with a different leader. These leaders often hired personal musicians whom they considered to be servants. The musicians were not free to come and go as they pleased. Johann Sebastian's first long-term employment was under the Duke of Saxe-Weimar where he worked for nine years. During this time, he visited the court of Dresden. While he was there, a famous French organist was also visiting. The Frenchman was said to be the best organist of his time and a competition was set up between them. The day before the competition, the French organist sneaked in to hear Bach practice. He was so impressed with Bach's abilities on the organ that he left in the middle of the night, and Johann Sebastian was declared the winner without an official competition.

When Bach decided to leave this post with the Duke for a job working for Prince Leopold, the Duke was not happy and held him as prisoner for a month. However, since Bach's new employer was a prince, the Duke was forced to release Bach. Bach greatly enjoyed working for Prince Leopold, who was also a talented musician and enjoyed making music with his musicians.

In 1720 Johann Sebastian's wife died while he was away. In December of the following year, he remarried to a professional singer, Anna Magdalena Wilcken. She was about half his age, but she was a good mother to her stepchildren and an invaluable help to her new husband. Together they had another 13 children, giving Bach a total of 20 children. However, life in those days was hard and only seven of the children made it to adulthood. Of these seven, only five lived to old age.

Johann Sebastian Bach was not only considered the best organist of his time, but he was also considered a top organ builder. He was often asked to design and build special organs. He was also a great composer and wrote over 1,000 compositions, though few were published during his lifetime. His second wife and his children were very instrumental in helping him write down many of his compositions.

When Bach died, his music lay silent for about 100 years and was almost lost to us, until a 20-year-old musician named Mendelssohn saved it. Today, Bach's music is well known and loved around the world. Most of what was written for the organ is now played on the piano. And now some of Johann Sebastian Bach's music is on the Voyager Space Probe reaching into outer space.

Despite his many achievements, we must not forget however, that most of Bach's music was written as worship music to God and is still used to glorify Him today. He once wrote, "The aim and final end of all music should be none other than the glory of God and the refreshment of the soul."

Front page of the autograph of Sonata for single violin #1 in E minor by Johann Sebastian Bach

UNIT 6

LIGHT

LIGHT

It's bright!

LESSON 28

What are some properties of light?

Words to know:

incandescent

fluorescent

LED

Challenge words:

transparent

translucent

opaque

umbra

penumbra

Have you ever been in a very dark room? It's usually a relief to turn on the light so you can see around you. Light is a very important part of our lives. Like sound, light is energy that travels in waves. However, light waves do not need a medium through which to travel. Light can and does travel through the vacuum of space.

Light waves with a frequency between 4.0×10^{14} and 7.5×10^{14} Hz are visible to the human eye and are thus called visible light. The color of visible light with the lowest frequency is red light. The highest frequency light that is visible is violet light. Other colors of light have frequencies in between these colors. White light is a combination of all colors of light and thus there is not a frequency that corresponds to white light. Some animals have a different range of vision from people and can actually see infrared or ultraviolet light that humans cannot see.

The primary source of light on earth is the sun. The sun's diameter is about 100 times bigger than the earth's diameter. It is approximately 93 million miles (150 million kilometers) from the earth. The sun is constantly releasing huge amounts of energy, only some of which is in the form of visible light. Only 1/1000th of 1/1,000,000th of the light, heat, and other energy produced by the sun ever reaches the surface of the earth. Yet, this is enough energy to light and warm up our world, and allow the plants to produce the food necessary for nearly all life on earth. This is evidence of God's design and care for our world.

Light travels much faster than sound. The speed of light depends on the medium through which it is traveling. Light travels fastest through a vacuum

APPRECIATING LIGHT

Purpose: To appreciate light

Materials: boxes or chairs, blindfold

Procedure:

1. Make a maze using boxes, chairs, or other objects.

2. Blindfold each person and have him/her navigate the maze. Assist the person going through the maze, if necessary.

3. After completing the maze, allow the person to go through the maze without a blindfold

and with enough light to see. It will be much easier. Light certainly is a great blessing from God.

OPTIONAL—CANDLE MAKING

A fun way to make your own light is to make homemade candles. Materials for this can be obtained from a craft store.

at about 186,000 miles/sec (300,000,000 m/s). It takes light waves approximately 8.3 minutes to travel from the sun to the earth. Light slows down just slightly as it travels through the air, but it travels even slower through water, at about 138,000 miles/sec (223,000,000 m/s), and through glass, at about 124,000 miles/sec (200,000,000 m/s).

How bright a light source appears to be is determined by two factors: how much energy is generated by the source and the distance you are from the source. Although the sun is not the biggest or brightest star in the universe, it certainly appears much brighter to the people of earth than any other star because it is much closer to the earth than any other star.

Although the sun is the primary source of light on earth, it is not the only source. Man has developed many ways to create light. Some of the earliest man-made sources of light were flames from candles, oil lamps, and gas lamps. But today, most man-made light comes from various kinds of light bulbs. Incandescent light bulbs are bulbs that contain filaments made from a material such as tungsten, which emits light when electrical current is passed through it. Thomas Edison constructed the first working incandescent light bulb. Fluorescent bulbs contain a gas that becomes a plasma when current is passed through it. The plasma emits ultraviolet light. The inside of the bulb is coated with a phosphor coating that glows when it is hit by ultraviolet light. The word fluorescent comes from the element fluorite. Fluorite is a substance that glows under ultraviolet light; however, fluorite is not generally used to make the phosphors that glow inside fluorescent light bulbs. Fluorescent lights are usually more efficient than

FUN FACT

Some animals produce light through a process called bioluminescence. This is a chemical reaction that takes place in the animal's body and produces light.

Light

incandescent bulbs—they produce more light for a given amount of electricity. Until recently, fluorescent bulbs have been larger and more expensive to install, so incandescent lights have been common in most homes; however, newer technology has made smaller fluorescent bulbs available that can replace incandescent bulbs in many places.

The newest type of light is the LED or light-emitting diode. An LED is a small bulb containing a semiconductor that emits light when current is passed through it. LEDs are even more efficient that fluorescent bulbs. LEDs are now being used in many cities for traffic signals and even for Christmas lights. ■

WHAT DID WE LEARN?

- How is a light wave different from a sound wave?
- Name three sources of light.
- Which color of light has the lowest frequency? The highest frequency?
- Explain how incandescent bulbs, fluorescent bulbs, and LEDs produce light.

TAKING IT FURTHER

- Why do people say that life on earth depends on sunlight?
- Why do some stars appear brighter than others in the night sky?

SHADOWS

Light waves can pass through some materials and not through others. **Transparent** materials allow all light to pass through. Most glass is transparent. Materials that allow some light to pass through, but block other light, are said to be **translucent**. Smoked or colored glass is translucent. **Opaque** materials block all light. Most solid objects are opaque.

Opaque objects will cast a shadow. A shadow is the area where the light is blocked. Shadows consist of two parts. The part in the center that is black is called the **umbra**. No light shines in the umbra. A small amount of light shines around the edges of an object, causing a gray area around the umbra. This is called the **penumbra**. The amount of umbra and penumbra varies depending on how focused the light source is and the distance the object is from the light source. A very focused light will create a shadow with very little to no penumbra. A diffuse light source will create a larger penumbra.

Purpose: To experiment with shadows

Materials: desk lamp, book

Procedure:

1. Shine a desk lamp onto a wall.

2. Place a book in the light and observe the shadow. The umbra, or black area of the shadow, should be easy to see. Can you see any penumbra, or gray area around the shadow?

3. Move the book closer to and farther from the lamp. How does this affect the shadow?

COLOR

Red or blue?

Why do things have different colors?

Words to know:

prism

retina

rods

cones

When you hear the word *light*, you probably think of white light. Visible light often appears to be white, but there is no wavelength of energy that corresponds to white light. Instead, white light actually consists of all the colors of light combined together. One of the first people to prove that white light consists of many colors of light was Sir Isaac Newton, in 1665. Newton was very interested in light, and he tested light in many ways. He developed a specially-shaped piece of glass called a prism. Newton used the prism to show that white light is actually composed of many different colors of light.

To understand how a prism works, you need to remember that light travels faster through air than it does through water or glass. As light enters glass it slows down, and different colors of light slow down different amounts as they go through the glass. Red light travels more quickly through glass than violet light does.

So although all the colors of light enter the prism together, they do not exit together. The different colors of light are actually bent a slight amount with each color being bent a different amount; so the light leaving the prism is diffused or spread out and you can actually see each color of light separately. This produces a rainbow effect. In fact, this is precisely how rainbows are produced. Sunlight passes through water drops in the sky. This light is refracted or split as it travels through the water drops and emerges in the various colors of the rainbow. That's how we see God's promise as a beautiful rainbow in the sky.

You are able to distinguish different colors because God created your eyes to be able to detect different wavelengths of light. The retina is the back part of the eye. It is covered with special light-detecting cells. Some of these cells are called rods

SPLITTING LIGHT

Purpose: To see the different colors of light

Materials: prism, shallow dish, hand mirror

Procedure:

1. If you have a prism, place it so that sunlight shines through it onto a wall.

2. If you do not have a prism, place a shallow dish of water on a flat surface where the sun will shine into the water.

3. Hold a hand mirror in the water so that the light passing through the water hits the mirror and is reflected onto the wall. You should be able to see all of the colors of the light reflected onto the wall.

4. Use the mirror to reflect sunlight onto the wall without the light first passing through the water. How is the light different from that which passed through the water? The different colors of light become separated as they pass through the water or through the glass of the prism.

COMBINING LIGHT

Purpose: To understand how you see white light when all colors of light are present

Materials: bowl or small plate, white paper, scissors, ruler, pencil, colored markers

Procedure:

1. Trace around a bowl or small plate to make a circle on white paper that is about 5 inches across.

2. Cut out the circle.

3. Use a ruler and pencil to divide the paper into six equal sections, like pieces of a pie.

4. Use markers to color each section of the circle. The first section should be red, the next orange, then yellow, green, blue, and purple.

5. Take a sharp pencil and push it through the center of the circle to form a top.

6. Spin the top and watch the colors of the circle as they blend together.

Conclusion: The circle will appear to be nearly white as long as all of the colors are reaching your eye simultaneously. Once the circle begins to slow down, your eyes will be able to again distinguish the separate colors.

Light

because of their long thin shape. Rods detect even small amounts of light, allowing you to see in darkened rooms. Other cells are cone-shaped and are called **cones**. These cells detect different wavelengths of light and allow you to distinguish between various colors. Both kinds of cells are light sensitive and produce a chemical reaction that creates an electrical signal that is sent to the brain.

Most objects do not produce any light themselves, yet we are able to see them because of the light that they reflect. Each material absorbs some wavelengths of light and reflects the others. This is why objects appear to be different colors even though the same light is hitting each object. The wavelengths of light that are reflected are those that correspond to the color of the object. For example, an object that appears to be purple is absorbing all wavelengths of light except those corresponding to purple light. Objects that appear to be white reflect all wavelengths of light and those that appear to be black absorb all wavelengths of light.

When you look around you, you will be amazed at the wide variety of colors that God placed in the world for our enjoyment. ■

WHAT DID WE LEARN?

- What is the true color of white light?
- Why does light split when it goes through glass or water?
- How do our eyes detect light?
- What color of light does a yellow object absorb?

TAKING IT FURTHER

- Why does light appear to be white instead of all different colors?
- How can we see objects when they do not produce light?
- How can we see black objects if they do not reflect any light?

FILTERS

We can control the color of light an object produces by using filters. Colored filters allow only one color or wavelength of light to pass through. This in turn can change the color that an object appears to be. If only red light hits a white object, it may appear to be red because it can only reflect the red light. Use a flashlight and colored filters or colored plastic to complete the "What Color Will It Be?" worksheet.

Light

REFLECTION

Bouncing back

LESSON 30

How does light reflect off surfaces?

Words to know:

reflection

angle of incidence

angle of reflection

Take a look in the mirror. What do you see? Do you see someone who looks just like you only backwards? When you raise your hand, the person in the mirror raises his/her hand. This phenomenon is called **reflection**. We are very familiar with reflections in a mirror. But just how does this phenomenon work?

Light waves travel in straight lines and are thus called rays of light. Rays of light continue in a straight line until they encounter an object. When the light hits an object, the light is either absorbed or bounces off of the object. This bouncing light is called a reflection. As you learned in the previous lesson, we see objects because of the light that is reflected off of them.

Because light travels only in straight lines, it will reflect off of a smooth flat surface, such as a mirror, at the same angle that it hits the surface. The angle formed between the light ray that approaches the mirror and a line perpendicular to the mirror is called the **angle of incidence**. Look at the diagram below. You can see that the angle of incidence in this example is 45 degrees. The angle formed between the light ray that is leaving the mirror and the normal, or perpendicular line, is called the **angle of reflection**. In the drawing, you see that the angle of reflection is also 45 degrees.

When we think of reflections, we generally think of a mirror. But to varying degrees, light reflects off of nearly any surface. Nearly all of the light that hits a

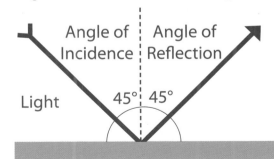

Angle of Incidence | Angle of Reflection

Light

45° 45°

Light

REFLECTING LIGHT

Most mirrors have a silvery coating on the back, which reflects the light that hits it.

Purpose: To test which materials would make the best mirrors

Materials: aluminum foil, flashlight, white paper, black paper

Procedure:

1. Place a smooth piece of aluminum foil on a smooth surface near a wall.

2. Shine a flashlight onto the foil at an angle. You should see a reflection of the flashlight beam on the wall.

3. Next, crumple another piece of foil then spread it out and set it next to the smooth foil. It should not be perfectly flat.

4. Again, shine the flashlight on the foil. How does the reflection on the wall compare to that from the smooth foil?

5. Repeat your test using white paper instead of aluminum foil. How does the reflection compare to the reflection from the smooth foil? Why?

6. Again, repeat the test using non-shiny black paper. How does this reflection compare to the others?

smooth shiny surface will be reflected. This surface could be a mirror, or it could be a still lake or pond. It could even be a shiny bumper or a window on the car in front of you. Surfaces that are not smooth or shiny may only reflect a small amount of light. ∎

Light reflects off of glass and water like a mirror.

Light

WHAT DID WE LEARN?

- What is a reflection?
- Which types of materials best reflect light?
- What kind of path does light take?

TAKING IT FURTHER

- If light approaches a mirror at a 30-degree angle of incidence, what will the angle of reflection be?
- If the back of a mirror is not smooth, what is likely to happen to the image you see?

ANGLE OF INCIDENCE

Purpose: To show that the angle of incidence is equal to the angle of reflection

Materials: cardboard, pencil, protractor, modeling clay, hand mirror, flashlight, pins or tacks

Procedure:

1. Cut a thick piece of cardboard to be 12 inches by 16 inches.

2. Draw a line across the cardboard about two inches from the narrow end of the board.

3. Draw a second line down the middle of the cardboard to form a cross shape on the board.

4. Using a protractor, draw a line that forms a 15-degree angle with the center line, a 45-degree line, and a 60-degree line all to the left of the center as shown in the diagram.

5. Use modeling clay to fasten a small hand mirror so that it rests upright along the shorter line and is centered over the

longer line as shown in the diagram.

6. Turn off the lights in the room and place a flashlight so that it is pointing at the center of the mirror, shining along the 15-degree line. Use three pins or tacks to mark the line of the reflected light from the mirror.

7. Move the flashlight to shine on the mirror along the 45-degree line. Again, mark the path of the reflected light ray.

8. Finally, repeat this procedure for the 60-degree angle.

9. Turn on the lights, remove the mirror, and carefully remove the pins from the first flashlight beam.

10. Use a red marker and a ruler to draw a line connecting the holes made by the pins marking the first reflected ray.

11. Repeat, using a blue marker to mark the path of the second test and a green marker to

mark the path of the light from the third test.

12. Use a protractor to measure the angle of reflection for each test.

Questions:

- How did the angle of reflection compare with the angle of incidence for each test? Their measurements should be close.

- Why might the angles be slightly different?

- If your measurements are different by more than a few degrees, what might be the explanation?

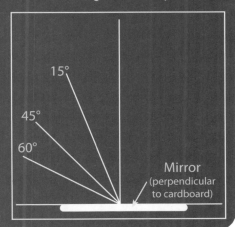

15°

45°

60°

Mirror
(perpendicular
to cardboard)

Light

MIRRORS

Mirror, mirror on the wall

LESSON 31

How do different mirrors reflect light differently?

Words to know:

plane mirror

virtual image

concave mirror

convex mirror

Smooth glass with a shiny coating on the back is a great reflector of light. We call this a mirror. With a flat mirror, called a **plane mirror**, the reflected light allows you to see an image that appears to be behind the surface of the mirror. This image is backward from what an actual image would be. For example, if you were looking in a mirror and you raised your right hand, the image would raise his/her hand on that same side, what we would consider to be the left hand if someone were really behind the mirror. If you move back from the mirror, the image appears to move backward, farther behind the mirror. Since there really isn't anything behind the mirror, the reflected image is called a **virtual image**.

Not all mirrors are flat or plane mirrors. Many reflective surfaces are curved. Have you ever been to a carnival or museum and walked past a curved mirror that made you laugh at your distorted reflection? Curved mirrors change the reflection you would see in a plane mirror. These surfaces can be curved either away from or toward the incoming light. If the surface is curved away from the light (the center of the mirror is inward, like a cave), it is called a **concave mirror**. If it is curved toward the light (or outward), it is called a **convex mirror**.

Concave mirrors bend light toward the center. Parallel light rays hit the surface of the concave mirror at different angles since the surface of the mirror is curved. Therefore, each ray leaves at a different angle.

FUN FACT

When it's finally completed in 2016, the Giant Magellan Telescope will be the largest telescope in the world, consisting of seven 27.6-feet (8.4-meter) mirrors aligned to work as a single mirror 84 feet (25.6 m) across—with 10 times the resolution of the Hubble Space Telescope.

Light

CONVEX OR CONCAVE?

Purpose: To identify the difference between the images projected by different types of mirrors

Materials: flat mirror, spoon

Procedure:

1. Look at your own reflection in a regular, plane mirror.

2. Now look at your image reflected in the bowl of a shiny spoon. How is the image different? The reflection in the spoon is upside down and smaller than the image in the plane mirror. Also, your chin may be stretched and your forehead shortened. The bowl of the spoon is a concave mirror.

3. Now turn the spoon around and look at your reflection in the back of the spoon. The back of the spoon is a convex mirror. How does this image compare to the image in the plane mirror? It is right side up but it is stretched and distorted.

4. Move the spoon closer and farther away. How does this affect the image?

5. Hold the spoon at different angles, to the side, or up and

down. How does this affect the image?

Conclusion: The curvature of the spoon causes the light rays to reflect at different angles than you are used to seeing in a plane mirror so the image is distorted.

FUN FACT

To help you remember the names of the different types of mirrors, you can remember that a cave goes into the side of a mountain, and a concave mirror curves inward, away from the light.

The curve of the mirror causes the rays to converge at a point near the center of the mirror. The image is also inverted, or turned upside down, by the concave mirror.

Concave mirrors are used in reflecting telescopes. The mirrors collect parallel light from distant stars and focus it into a bright image. Concave mirrors are also found in flashlights and spotlights. The mirror around the bulb concentrates the light rays into a single bright beam. This same idea is used to make automobile headlights brighter and more focused.

Convex mirrors are curved outward and thus reflect the incoming light outward. This causes an image to appear stretched and bigger than normal. Makeup mirrors are often slightly convex to allow you to see your face in more detail. Also, rear view and side mirrors on cars are often convex. This allows you to see a wider area than you would with a plane mirror.

Mirrors of all kinds—plane, concave, and convex—are used in many applications. In addition to those already listed, mirrors are used in periscopes,

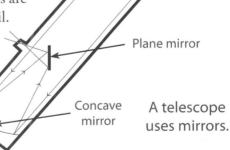

Plane mirror

Concave mirror

A telescope uses mirrors.

Light

kaleidoscopes, dental and surgical lights, and often in microscopes as well. You may be most familiar with your bathroom mirror, but if you pay attention, you may find many other uses for mirrors other than helping you see to comb your hair. ■

WHAT DID WE LEARN?

- What are the three shapes of mirrors?
- How does a concave mirror affect light rays and the reflected image?
- How does a convex mirror affect the light rays and the reflected image?

TAKING IT FURTHER

- Would you expect the reflected image from a concave mirror to be brighter or darker than the original image?
- Explain how a periscope uses mirrors.

PERISCOPE UP

You can have fun with mirrors by making your own periscope. Use cardboard and tape to form a tube. Place one mirror at the top of the tube and one at the bottom so that the top mirror reflects light to the bottom mirror and out the periscope to your eye (see diagram).

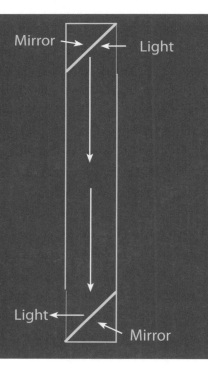

Light

REFRACTION

Bending the light

How can light be bent?

Words to know:

refraction

mirage

When light passes from one medium to another, it changes speed. Light travels more quickly through air than it does through water or glass. When the light changes speed, it is bent and travels at a different angle through the new medium than it traveled originally. This bending of light is called refraction. It is important to remember that light travels in straight lines. So when we say that light is bent, we don't mean that it begins to move in a curve. The light still travels in a straight line once it enters the new medium; it just travels in a different direction at a different angle.

Refraction of light can cause many optical illusions. For example, if you are looking at an item under water, it will appear to be farther away than it actually is because the light slows down as it enters the water and is reflected back to your eye at a different angle than you expect. A spear fisherman or a grizzly bear trying to capture a fish must compensate for this phenomenon and aim closer to shore than the fish appears to be.

Another effect of refraction occurs during hot summer days. The sun heats dark materials on the ground such as asphalt or sand, causing the surrounding

A mirage

Light

OBSERVING REFRACTION

Purpose: To observe refraction

Materials: clear drinking cup, pencil, small flashlight or laser pen, milk

Procedure:

1. Fill a clear drinking cup ¾ full of water.

2. Place a pencil in the cup and observe the pencil from the side of the cup.

3. Remove the pencil and add a small amount of milk to the water. This will help make the beam more visible.

4. Darken the room.

5. Shine a beam of light down into the water from above the surface at an angle, not straight down. A flashlight with a very concentrated beam or a laser pen works best. Observe the angle that the light enters the water and the angle that the light travels through the water.

6. Next, shine the light into the water from the side so that it passes through the glass or plastic of the container first.

Questions:

• How did the pencil in the water look from the side of the cup? Why?

• How was the light bent when entering from the top of the cup?

• Was it bent the same or different when entering through the side of the cup? If it was different, why was it different?

Conclusion: The pencil looked crooked or bent in the cup of water. Obviously, the pencil is straight. But it appears bent because the light rays are bent as they pass through the water and the glass. Thus, the rays hit our eyes in a location that is different than you expect, so the pencil appears to be bent. The light beam was bent differently when entering from the side of the cup because it also passed through the glass or plastic, which would cause a different amount of refraction.

air to become very warm. As light passes from cooler denser air into the warmer less dense air near the ground it speeds up and is refracted. This causes an image of the sky to be projected above the ground, making it appear that there is water shimmering on the ground. This phenomenon is called a mirage.

Refracted light is often used by illusionists to trick people into thinking they see something that they are not really seeing. But more often refracted light is used

FUN FACT

Refraction causes the sun to appear to rise slightly earlier and to set slightly later than it otherwise would if the light were not bent by the earth's atmosphere.

in technology to help us see things that we would not be able to see otherwise. For example, light is refracted through lenses in cameras, microscopes, binoculars, and telescopes to help us see images that we would not otherwise be able to see, because they are too small or too far away. We will study more about lenses in the next lesson. ■

WHAT DID WE LEARN?

- What is refraction?
- Why do items appear to be in a different location underwater than they actually are?
- What is a mirage?

TAKING IT FURTHER

- Will light bend more or less as it passes through a denser material than through a less dense material?
- Are you more likely to see a mirage during the summer or the winter? Why?

DENSITY AND REFRACTION

Purpose: To compare refraction for three liquids

Materials: three containers, milk, salt, vegetable oil, flashlight

Now we are going to repeat the activity experiment using three liquids with different densities.

Procedure:

1. Pour 1 cup of water into the first container and add a small amount of milk to it.

2. Pour 1 cup of water into the second container and add a small amount of milk. Also, add 3 tablespoons of salt to this container.

3. Pour 1 cup of vegetable oil into a third container.

4. Darken the room and shine the light beam into the milky water from above the surface of the water. Observe the angle of refraction.

5. Next, shine the light at the same angle into the salty water. How is the angle of refraction different?

6. Finally, shine the light into the vegetable oil. How does the angle of refraction compare to what you observed in the other two liquids?

7. For an interesting show, carefully pour the fresh water on top of the salt water. Next, carefully pour the oil on top of the water. Now shine your light into the mixture and see what happens. You should be able to observe multiple refractions if the liquids form distinct layers.

Questions:

- Which substance bent the light the most? Which substance bent the light the least?
- What are the relative densities of the three liquids?
- How does density appear to affect the refraction of light?

Light

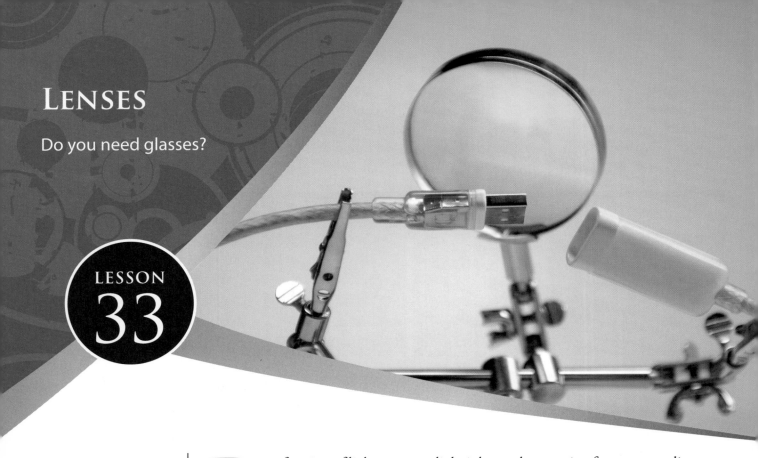

LENSES

Do you need glasses?

LESSON 33

How do different lenses affect how we see?

Words to know:

concave lens

convex lens

focal point

principal focus

focal length

diverging lens

Refraction of light occurs as light is bent when passing from one medium to another. Lenses are specially curved pieces of glass or plastic that are used to bend or refract light for particular purposes. If the lens curves inward, like a cave, it is a concave lens. If it curves outward, it is a convex lens. These are the same terms that are used to describe curved mirrors.

As parallel beams of light pass through a convex lens, one with sides that curve outward, the rays are all bent toward the center. The point at which the beams converge is called the focal point or the principal focus. The distance from the lens to the focal point is called the focal length of the lens. The focal length is determined by the curve and thickness of the lens, as well as by the material the lens is made from.

An image that is produced by a convex lens is called a real image because it can be projected onto another surface. Depending on the focal length of the lens and the distance the object is from the lens, the image may be larger and right side up, or it may be smaller and upside down.

Concave lenses, ones that are curved inward, cause parallel beams of light to bend outward as they pass through the lens. This type of lens is sometimes referred to as a diverging lens. A concave lens produces a virtual image, one that cannot be projected. This image is always smaller and right side up.

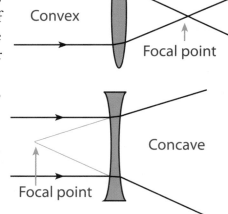

Convex

Focal point

Concave

Focal point

HOMEMADE CAMERA

Purpose: To make your own "camera" with a few simple materials

Materials: cardboard tube, small box, pencil, scissors, tape, tracing paper, magnifying glass

Procedure:

1. Place a cardboard tube upright in the center of one side of a small box and trace around the tube.

2. Cut out the circle and slide the tube a short distance into the hole and tape it in place.

3. Cut the opposite side of the box off completely.

4. Replace the side of the box with a sheet of tracing paper. Glue or tape the tracing paper in place.

5. Tape a magnifying glass onto the end of the cardboard tube.

6. Now you can point your camera at any well-lit object and see an image projected onto the tracing paper "film."

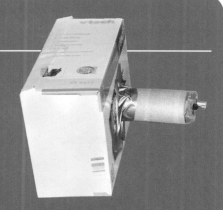

Questions: How does the image on the "film" compare to the actual object? Why is the image different from the real thing?

Lenses have many uses in today's world. However, the oldest useful lens was created by God. Each of your eyes contains a convex lens that projects an image onto the retina of your eye. Once man began to understand how light works, he began to invent uses for lenses as well. One of the earliest uses for lenses was in the telescope. Galileo is credited with inventing the first telescope. This device used two convex lenses. The lens at one end collected and concentrated the light to produce a clear image of the object being observed. The second lens magnified the image, making it easier to see. Today, many telescopes use a series of lenses or a combination of mirrors and lenses to gather distant light and allow us to better see the stars and planets.

A natural extension of using lenses for telescopes was to use lenses for microscopes. In a microscope, a light source or a mirror reflects light through the specimen being observed to a convex lens called the objective. This lens magnifies the image and shines the light through a second convex lens called the eyepiece, which further magnifies the image. Thus, a microscope allows us to see very small items, making them appear hundreds of times bigger than they actually are.

FUN FACT

An experiment was done where a man wore a pair of glasses that turned all the images upside down before they reached his eyes. After a few days, his brain compensated for this and objects appeared right side up when he had the glasses on. When he quit wearing the glasses, everything appeared upside down until his brain again learned to adjust. God has designed our bodies with an amazing ability to adapt.

Light

Another important use of lenses is in cameras. In simple terms, a film camera is a light-tight box with a very small hole in the front. The lens on the front of the camera gathers light and focuses it through the small hole and projects the image onto the film at the back of the camera. Digital cameras do not use film. Instead, the lens focuses the image onto an array of electrical devices called diodes. The diodes convert the light into electrical signals that can be stored in the camera's memory. A computer is then used to convert the stored data into an image that can be displayed. ■

WHAT DID WE LEARN?

- What is a lens?
- What effect does a convex lens have on light?
- What effect does a concave lens have on light?
- What is another name for a concave lens?
- Name three inventions that use lenses.

TAKING IT FURTHER

- Would you expect the image seen through a microscope to be right side up or upside down? What about the image seen through a telescope?
- The image projected onto your retina is upside down, so why don't you see things upside down?

FOCAL LENGTH

Using several different convex lenses, measure the focal length of each lens and complete the "Focal Length" worksheet.

EYES & EYEGLASSES

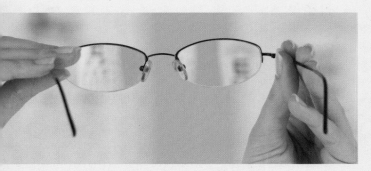

Eyeglasses are perhaps one of man's most useful inventions. These simple pieces of glass have enabled and extended our ability to see the wonderful world around us. When did man first start using lenses to help him see? It seems that the Romans didn't know about the power of lenses. A letter written by a prominent Roman around 100 BC states that he had resigned himself to old age where he could no longer read for himself but must have his slaves read for him.

Around AD 1000 something called a reading stone was used, mostly by monks. It was a glass sphere that was cut in two and laid on the reading material to magnify it. From these reading stones the Venetians learned how to produce glass lenses, which were held in frames in front of the eye or between the eye and the object being observed, somewhat like today's magnifying glass. Then in 1268, English Franciscan Friar Roger Bacon wrote that letters appeared larger when viewed through less than half a sphere of glass, a principle that had been described by Alhazen (965–1038), an Arabian mathematician, optician, and astronomer, as well as by earlier Greeks, but had not been acted upon.

All of these observations contributed to the earliest known eyeglasses which were made in 1286, from two convex-shaped lenses, each put into its own frame with a handle attached. No one knows who made the first pair, but they were an instant success. By the 1400s eyeglasses were cheap and plentiful and even most laborers could afford a pair if needed.

The main problem with early eyeglasses was that all the lenses were convex and could only help farsighted people. It was not until the 16th century that concave eyeglasses were developed. Pope Leo X was very nearsighted and wore concave spectacles when hunting.

To understand why convex or concave lenses help us see better, let's first look at the way the eye works. As the light from an object enters the eye, the convex lens at the front of the eyeball bends the light. The image is inverted, and the place where the image forms is called the focus point. In perfect sight, this point is on the retina at

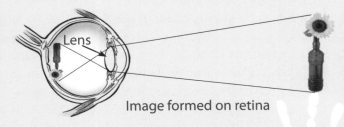

Lens

Image formed on retina

the back wall of the eye. The muscles on the eye pull on the lens, changing its shape and thus changing the focus. This ability is what allows us to see things clearly at far distances as well as close up.

However, not everybody's eyes focus correctly. Many people are farsighted. Being farsighted means that the lens in the eye is no longer convex enough to focus the image on the retina at the back of the eye. In this case, the focus point is beyond the eye. The farther back the focus point is the more out of focus the image will appear. Many times, if a person

Farsightedness

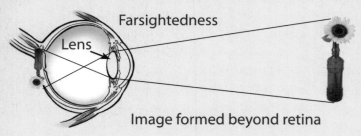

Image formed beyond retina

is only a little farsighted, he/she will try to hold the object farther away in order to see it more clearly. But in most cases, the arms become too short and the person has to get glasses to see clearly.

Some people have the opposite problem. This is when the lens in the eye is too convex and the focus point is in front of the retina. This is called being nearsighted. Nearsighted people can clearly see objects that are near, but distant objects are blurry.

Nearsightedness

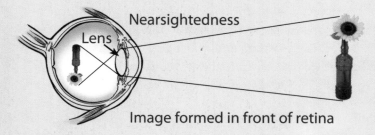

Image formed in front of retina

For most people these problems show up as they age because the lenses become less flexible. As the lens becomes more rigid, it becomes

harder for the eye muscles to change the shape of the lens and compensate for any imperfections in the lens.

However, man has discovered a way to fix these problems through the wonders of shaped glass or plastic. If the glass or plastic is shaped into a convex lens, as shown, the light will be bent inwards just in front of the lens in the eye. This will move the focus point closer to the lens and help compensate for farsightedness.

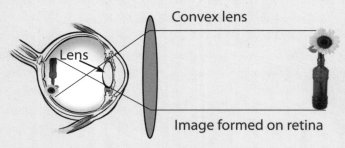

Convex lens

Image formed on retina

In a similar way, nearsightedness can be corrected by placing a concave lens just in front of the eye. This will bend the rays out just before they enter the eye, moving the focus point farther back in the eye.

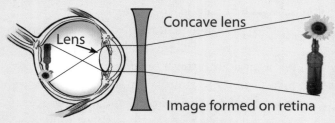

Concave lens

Image formed on retina

Today, many people are choosing to have laser surgery rather than wear glasses or contact lenses. A laser is used to reshape the eye's cornea and thus correct many vision problems.

One way to help your eyes, and perhaps delay some of these problems, is to change your point of focus on a regular basis. This can be done by changing from looking at something close to looking at something far away and back again. If you are spending a lot of your time reading or looking at a computer monitor, you should do this several times each hour. Remember, your eyes are very important.

USING ENERGY: FINAL PROJECT

Converting energy for our use

LESSON 34

What are the many ways that we use energy?

Let's review what we have learned about energy. Scientists define energy as the ability to perform work. There are many different forms of energy, including mechanical energy, chemical energy, nuclear energy, thermal energy, electricity (and magnetism), gravitational energy, sound, and light. And remember, all of these may be categorized as either kinetic or potential energy. If you need to, review what each kind of energy is and how it is used.

Remember, God is the source of all energy in the universe. The first law of thermodynamics states that energy and matter cannot be created or destroyed; they can only change form. So we know that all energy originally came from God at Creation. Look around you and see how that energy is being put to good use. ■

Light

FINAL PROJECT: MY ENERGY BOOK

If you have a camera, take pictures of energy at work. For example, take a picture of someone lifting a box or doing exercise. Take pictures of electrical appliances. Take pictures of lights, CD players, and cars. You can photograph anything that is using energy. If you do not have a camera, you can cut pictures from old magazines, or draw your own pictures.

Once you have a good collection of pictures of energy, make an energy book. Place each picture on a page and describe the energy being used. Describe what type of energy is used initially, what form it is converted into, and what the result of that energy is. Try to include as many different kinds of energy as you can find.

Have fun and be creative with your book. Be sure to include a cover and/or title page. You may want to group your pictures together according to the types of energy that the pictures show or according to the work that is being done. And don't forget to include a note about how nearly all energy on earth begins with the sun one way or another.

WHAT DID WE LEARN?

- What are some of the types of energy recognized by scientists?
- What two basic forms can energy be found to take?

TAKING IT FURTHER

- What is your favorite way to use energy?

ENERGY CHAINS

In your energy book, be sure to include complete energy chains for each picture. For example, for a picture of a light bulb you should start with the sun. Then show that the sun's light is transformed into chemical energy in plants. The plant becomes coal that is burned at the power plant where thermal energy is converted into mechanical energy, then to electromagnetic energy, and then to electricity. The electricity is finally converted into light and heat in the light bulb. Be sure to put some thought into the ultimate source and all conversions of energy for each picture.

Light

CONCLUSION

God gave us energy

How does God provide energy for us?

The second law of thermodynamics states that all systems move toward maximum entropy. This means that every system with energy in it moves toward a state of chaos or disorder. All of the energy in the universe will eventually be dissipated as heat or light. The earth is constantly losing energy to heat and light; however, God created the sun to provide the earth with new energy every day so that life can continue. This is a tremendous blessing.

Take a few minutes to read some Scripture verses that describe God's hand in providing energy for our world. Read Genesis 1 to see how God initially put all the matter and energy into the universe. Read Psalm 24:1–2 to see how God rules over everything on the earth. Read Isaiah 51:6 to see that the earth is wearing out. Finally, read 2 Peter 3:11–13 to see that God will use heat to destroy this earth and replace it with a new heaven and a new earth.

The ultimate power rests with God. Take some time to reflect on the blessings of energy and to honor Him for His love and care for us. ■

Light

GLOSSARY

Acoustics   A building's effect on sound

Amplitude   Difference between height of the peak and height of the center of the wave

Angle of incidence   Angle at which light approaches an object

Angle of reflection   Angle at which light reflects off of an object

Atomic bomb   Weapon powered by fission

Battery   Device that supplies electrons through a chemical reaction

Calorie   1,000 calories (Kilocalorie)

calorie   Amount of energy needed to raise 1 gram of water 1 degree Celsius

Cellular respiration/Digestion   Process that breaks down sugar molecules to release the stored energy

Chemical energy   Energy stored in chemical bonds

Circuit   Complete circular path that allows electrons to flow

Combustion   Releasing of energy through burning

Concave lens   Surfaces curve toward center of lens

Concave mirror   Surface is curved away from the incoming light

Conduction   Transferring of heat by the collision of particles

Cones   Special cells in the eye that detect different colors

Convection   Transferring of heat through currents

Convex lens/Diverging lens   Surfaces curve outward away from the center of the lens

Convex mirror   Surface is curved toward the incoming light

Current   Movement of electrons from an area of higher electrical potential to an area of lower electrical potential

Cycle   One complete wave

Diamagnetic/Nonmagnetic   Material that is unaffected by magnetic fields

Doppler effect   Pitch changes as an object moves toward or away from you

Electrical conductor   Material that allows electrons to flow easily

Electrical energy   Flow of electrons

Electrical insulator   Material that resists the flow of electrons

Electrical power   Voltage times current, a measure of how much current can be supplied in a given time period

Electromagnetic waves   Waves that can move through a vacuum

Electromagnet   Magnetic field generated by current flowing through a wire

Electronic instruments   Produce sound when electronic signals pass through a speaker

Electrons   Part of the atom with a negative electrical charge

Energy   Ability to perform work

Ferromagnetic   Material with a strong attraction to magnetic fields

Fission   Breaking apart of a nucleus into smaller nuclei

Fluorescent   Ultraviolet light emitted from plasma excites phosphors to produce light

Focal length   Distance from lens to focal point

Focal point/Principal focus   Point at which light rays converge

Fossil fuels   Petroleum products formed from the remains of plants and animals that were buried in the past and placed under pressure

Frequency   Number of peaks that pass a point in one second

Fusion   Combining of nuclear particles to form a larger nucleus

Gamma rays   Electromagnetic waves with frequencies above 1019 Hz

Generator   Mechanism for converting a changing magnetic field into a flow of current

Geothermal energy   Heat from inside the earth

Heat   Energy of moving atoms and molecules (see Thermal energy)

Hydrogen bomb/Thermonuclear bomb   Weapon powered by fusion

Incandescent   Emits light when current passes through a filament

Infrared radiation/Infrared waves   Electromagnetic waves with frequencies between microwaves and visible light

Ions   Electrically-charged particles

Kinetic energy   Energy that is being used

Law of charges   Opposite charges attract, similar charges repel

Law of magnetic poles   Opposite poles attract, similar poles repel

Light-emitting diode/LED   A small bulb containing a semiconductor that emits light when current is passed through it

Light energy   Electromagnetic waves that can be detected by the eye

Lightning   Sudden discharge of electricity

Loudness   Volume due to the energy/amplitude of the sound wave

Magnetic moment   Magnetic field generated by an electron

Magnetic north pole   Area on earth that magnetic materials align with

Magnetism   Attractive and repelling forces contained in magnetic materials

Mechanical energy   Energy of movement

Mechanical waves   Waves that must move through some physical medium such as air or water

Microwaves   Electromagnetic waves with frequencies between 109 and 1011 Hz

Mirage   Image of the sky projected above the ground because of different densities of air

Motor   Mechanism for converting changing current inside a magnetic field into mechanical energy

Neutrons   Part of the atom with a neutral electrical charge

Nuclear energy   Energy stored in the nucleus of an atom

Overtones/Harmonics   Vibrations that are multiples of the fundamental frequency

Parallel circuit   Circuit with multiple paths for current to flow

Paramagnetic   Material that has a slight effect on magnetic fields

Peak/Crest   Highest point of a wave

Percussion instruments   Produce sound when struck by an object

Photosynthesis   Reaction inside plants that combines water, carbon dioxide, and sunlight to produce sugar and oxygen

Pitch   Tone of sound due to the frequency of the sound wave

Plane mirror   Flat mirror

Potential energy   Energy that is stored

Power   Measure of how fast work can be accomplished

Prism   Glass that splits the colors of light

Protons   Part of the atom with a positive electrical charge

Radio waves   Electromagnetic waves with frequencies between 100 kHz and 100 MHz

Reflection   Wave changing direction when it bounces off a surface that does not absorb it

Refraction   Bending of light

Resistance   How much a material resists or slows down the flow of electrons

Resonance   Transferring of sound energy from one source to another

Retina   Back part of the eye

Reverberations   Multiple echoes

Rods   Special cells in the eye that detect light

SONAR   Use of sound waves to measure distance to an object

Semiconductor   Material that allows a small amount of electricity to flow

Serial circuit   Circuit with only one path for current to flow

Solar energy   Energy from the sun

Sound energy/Sound waves   Energy that travels in waves through matter such as air, water, or wood and can be detected by the human ear

Static electricity   Stationary electrical charge

String instruments   Produce sound by vibrating strings

Switch   Device to control the flow of electrons by opening and closing the circuit

Temperature   Average kinetic energy that an object's molecules possess

Thermal conductor   Material that easily conducts heat

Thermal energy   Total kinetic energy that an object's molecules possess (see Heat)

Thermal equilibrium   When two objects have reached the same temperature and no heat transfer is taking place

Thermal insulator   Material that does not easily conduct heat

Thermal radiation   Transferring of heat through electromagnetic waves

Thunder   Sonic boom caused by rapidly expanding air

Trough   Lowest point of a wave

Ultrasound   Mechanical waves above 20,000 Hz

Ultraviolet rays   Electromagnetic waves with frequencies just above the visible spectrum

Valence electrons   Outermost electrons in an atom

Van Allen belts   Donut-shaped magnetic fields surrounding the earth

Velocity   Speed at which the wave travels

Virtual image   Reflected image

Visible spectrum   Electromagnetic waves that are visible to the human eye

Voltage/Electrical potential   Electrical force that causes electrons to flow

Wavelength   Distance between two peaks

Waves   Rhythmic vibrations

Wind instruments   Produce sound when air is moved through them

X-rays   Electromagnetic waves with frequencies between 1016 and 1019 Hz

Challenge Glossary

Alpha particle   Two protons and two neutrons with no electrons

Analog signal   Information is transmitted as waves

Aurora australis   Southern lights

Aurora borealis   Northern lights

Aurora oval   The latitudes surrounding the poles in which auroras occur

Beta particle   Very high-speed electron

Bioenergy   Energy that comes from plant and animal matter

Constructive interference   When two waves combine to increase the amplitude of the wave

Destructive interference   When two waves cancel each other out

Digital signal   Information is transmitted as a series of pulses (1s and 0s)

First law of thermodynamics   Mass and energy cannot be created or destroyed; they can only change forms

Gamma radiation   Very energetic electromagnetic radiation

Heat of fusion   Energy required to melt a substance

Heat of vaporization   Energy required to turn a liquid into a gas

Integrated circuit   Electrical circuit built in semiconducting material

Interference   When two waves meet and affect each other

Longitudinal waves   Vibrations occur in the same direction that the wave moves

Opaque   Blocks all light

Penumbra   Gray area around umbra, small amount of light shining

Radioactive decay   Process whereby a nucleus releases radioactive particles and energy

Radioactive   Material with an unstable nucleus

Radiometric dating   Measuring the amount of radioactive elements in a substance to determine its age

Solar maximum   When sunspot activity is highest

Solar minimum   When sunspot activity is lowest

Thermal capacity/Specific heat   The ability of a substance to store or absorb heat

Transistor   A switch or gate that allows electricity to flow in a semiconductor

Translucent   Allows some light to pass and blocks other light

Transparent   Allows light to pass

Transverse waves   Waves travel at 90 degrees to the direction the vibration occurs

Umbra   Center of shadow, no light shining

INDEX